1980

Warships of the Royal Navy

Captain John E. Moore RN

WARSHIPS OF THE ROYAL NAVY

NAVAL INSTITUTE PRESS

Copyright © John E. Moore, 1979

Published and distributed in
the United States of America by
the Naval Institute Press
Annapolis, Maryland 21402

Printed in Great Britain

ISBN 0-87021-978-2
Library of Congress Catalog Card No. 79-84202

Photograph Credits
All photographs C & S Taylor except:
Vickers (Shipbuilding) Ltd, pages 22 and 23
MoD (Navy), pages 34 and 35, 51, 52 and 53
    55, 124 and 125

Contents

Introduction

Having decided at the age of thirteen to join the Royal Navy the next thing was to learn more about it. For this purpose I bought a copy of Dr Oscar Parkes' *Ships of the Royal Navy* little thinking that forty-three years later I should be editing this new book, its lineal successor. Looking at that original volume and studying the contents one is reminded very much of the astonishing changes which have taken place since 1935. The twenty battleships and battle-cruisers then listed carried heavy guns with a range of some twenty miles and a system of control archaic by modern standards. The six true aircraft-carriers had recently been re-fitted with arrester wires and *Glorious* had received the first 'accelerator' to assist aeroplanes in their take-off. The embarked aircraft were flown by pilots of the Royal Air Force, other aircrew were naval and the maintenance staff on board belonged to the RAF. This hotch-potch arrangement operated the Fairey Seal spotter reconnaissance aircraft and the Flycatcher fighter with a top speed of 133mph. By 1935 these were being replaced by the Swordfish torpedo bomber, Sea Gladiators, Skuas and Rocs – none with a particularly high performance.

Fifty-one cruisers and light-cruisers emphasised the need for trade protection while 168 destroyers were deployed to the main fleets based in the Home Fleet, in the Mediterranean and China with squadrons operating in the East and West Indies, South Africa, the Persian Gulf, New Zealand and South America. Backed by the navies of the Commonwealth countries this meant a world-wide deployment, yet five years later in 1940 Great Britain and the Commonwealth, backed only by those Allied ships that had escaped the German advance, were facing desperate problems against the far smaller navies of Hitler and Mussolini.

Today the Royal Navy forms part of the integrated naval forces of NATO and, except for occasional foreign deployments, is concentrated in the North East Atlantic. The ships of the Royal Navy have changed beyond recognition from those I knew when I joined the fleet in 1939. They are much smaller because modern missiles require less space. Their radar equipment would have amazed the three Radio Direction Finding operators in my first ship which was one of two in the navy with RDF. Steam or diesel were the only means of propulsion with the modern nuclear plants and gas-turbine engines twenty or more years in the future. Sonar was confined to short-range Asdic sets while depth charges were the only form of attack weapon – even the Squid was ten years ahead. Communications were simple, the sets huge by modern standards. Except for a very few of the more favoured capital ships all bridges were open and the 'operations room' consisted of a wall chart and a simple plotting table which, in many destroyers, was tucked into a corner of the wheelhouse, a convenient repository for kettles, cups and tins of cocoa. The submarines hunted by these ships had a maximum dived speed of 9 knots, a diving depth rarely more than 350 feet and a battery capacity which was only sufficient for a day's patrol, requiring the boat to surface by night to charge.

Prices were, by today's standards, very low. *Rodney* cost a fraction over £7.5 million compared with the possible £200 million for the new *Invincible* of about half her tonnage. The average price of the 10,000 ton 'County' class cruisers was under £2 million, while the 'Counties' of 1962-70 ranged between £14 and £17 million. Destroyers came at around £320,000 while the 'Sheffield' class, three times their tonnage, now cost in the region of £25 million. Submarine prices show an even greater discrepancy with the 'T' class of the 1935 Estimates being put in commission for £350,000 while today's 'Swiftsure' class runs out at around £35 million. Finally the minesweepers of the 850-ton 'Halcyon' class were fine vessels at £100,000 apiece – the new 'Hunt' class of MCM vessels of 725 tons will probably cost £12-£15 million each. So far as inflation is concerned these comparative figures may be said to be worthless but, when similar motor cars have increased their price tag by ten to fifteen times since 1935 an increase of one hundred times is, in part a measure of the extreme complexity of modern ships' equipment combined with the very high cost of research and development and the results of continual alterations and industrial problems in shipyards and component factories.

Thus the fleet displayed in the following pages is vastly different from that of 1935. The major warships of only the Home Fleet of that time much out-numbered the whole of the main strength of the Royal Navy today but the standard of training of the 71,500 men and 4000 women who man today's fleet is necessarily of a totally different standard from that achieved by the 121,000 of forty years ago. The revolution in training of the last few years has resulted in an objective approach hitherto unknown. Shore-aids and the streaming of people to various types of training, the use of task-books and improved pre-joining training have all contributed to a new high standard which, despite some drafting turbulence amongst very junior ratings who are still making their decisions, is resulting in a very professional body of men and women. The ships and the equipment they are called on to operate are the reflection of a great deal of thought by the Naval Staff and designers who are continually wracked by the Treasury's cry of 'What we can afford' rather than the planners' 'What we need'. The Royal Navy is in strong and capable hands and it remains for our politicians to acknowledge our maritime needs when the threats from without are greater than they have been for two hundred years.

J. E. Moore, Captain RN
October 1978

Organisation

Admiralty Board

Minister of State: Ministry of Defence (Vice-Chairman) and Minister of State for Defence Procurement:
  Dr J. W. Gilbert, MP
Parliamentary Under-Secretary of State for Defence for the Royal Navy:
  Dr Patrick Duffy, MP
Chief of the Naval Staff and First Sea Lord:
  Admiral Sir Terence Lewin, GCB, MVO, DSC, ADC
Chief of Naval Personnel and Second Sea Lord:
  Admiral Sir Gordon Tait, KCB, DSC
Controller of the Navy:
  Admiral Sir Richard Clayton, KCB
Chief of Fleet Support:
  Vice-Admiral J. H. F. Eberle
Vice-Chief of the Naval Staff:
  Vice-Admiral Sir Anthony Morton, KCB

Commanders-in-Chief

Commander-in-Chief, Naval Home Command:
  Admiral Sir David Williams, GCB, ADC
Commander-in-Chief, Fleet:
  Admiral Sir Henry Leach, KCB

Flag Officers

Flag Officer Naval Air Command:
  Vice Admiral D. A. Cassidi
Flag Officer, Carriers and Amphibious Ships:
  Rear-Admiral W. D. M. Staveley
Flag Officer, Sea Training:
  Rear-Admiral G. I. Pritchard
Flag Officer, Gibraltar:
  Rear-Admiral, M. L. Stacey
Flag Officer, Malta:
  Rear-Admiral O. N. A. Cecil
Flag Officer, Medway:
  Rear-Admiral C. B. Williams, OBE
Flag Officer, Plymouth:
  Vice-Admiral J. M. Forbes
Flag Officer, Portsmouth:
  Rear-Admiral W. J. Graham
Flag Officer, Scotland and Northern Ireland:
  Vice-Admiral C. Rusby, MVO

General Officers, Royal Marines

Commandant-General, Royal Marines
  Lieutenant-General J. C. C. Richards
Chief of Staff to Commandant-General. Royal Marines:
  Major-General R. P. W. Wall, CB
Major-General Training Group, Royal Marines:
  Major-General P. L. Spurgeon
Major-General Commando Forces, Royal Marines:
  Major-General Sir Steuart Pringle

Diplomatic Representation

British Naval Attaché in Bonn:
  Captain B. R. Outhwaite·
British Naval Adviser in Canberra:
  Captain P. A. Pinkster
British Naval Attaché in Moscow:
  Captain P. H. Coward
British Naval Adviser in Ottawa:
  Captain A. A. Hensher, MBE
British Naval Attaché in Paris:
  Captain W. S. Gueterbock
British Naval Attaché in Rome:
  Captain G. J. Byers
British Naval Attaché in Washington:
  Rear-Admiral R. M. Burgoyne

Personnel (including Royal Marines)

(a) 1973: 77,600 (10,200 officers, 67,400 ratings and ORs) plus 3600 servicewomen
    1974: 74,700 (10,200 officers, 64,500 ratings and ORs) plus 3600 servicewomen
    1975: 72,500 (10,000 officers, 62,500 ratings and ORs) plus 3700 servicewomen
    1976: 72,300 (9900 officers, 62,300 ratings and ORs) plus 3900 servicewomen
    1977: 72,200 (9800 officers, 62,400 ratings and ORs) plus 3900 servicewomen
    1978: 71,500 (9600 officers, 61,900 ratings and ORs) plus 4000 servicewomen
(b) Voluntary service
(c) RNR (1978): 2234 officers, 3208 ratings
(d) RMR (1978): 64 officers, 913 men

Fleet Disposition

First Flotilla (Rear-Admiral R. R. Squires)
Blake (Flag), 4 'County' class, 4 Frigate Squadrons: 1st (*Galatea* + 5 frigates), 2nd (*Apollo* + 5 frigates), 5th *(Hermione* + 1 destroyer and 4 frigates), 6th *(Sirius* + 1 destroyer and 5 frigates)

Second Flotilla (Rear-Admiral M. La T. Wemyss)
Tiger (Flag), 3 'County' class, 4 Frigate Squadrons: 3rd *(Diomede* + 1 destroyer and 4 frigates), 4th *(Cleopatra* + 4 frigates), 7th *(Jupiter* + 4 frigates), 8th *Ajax* + 5 frigates).

Submarine Command (Rear-Admiral J. D. E. Fieldhouse) HQ at Northwood:
1st Squadron *(Dolphin,* Portsmouth) 8 Patrol Submarines, 2nd Squadron (Devonport) 5 Fleet Submarines, 2 Patrol Submarines: 3rd Squadron *(Neptune,* Faslane) 3 Fleet

Submarines, 2 Patrol Submarines: 10th
Squadron *(Neptune,* Faslane) 3 SSBN

MCM Commands:
1st Squadron (Rosyth), 2nd Squadron
(Portsmouth), 3rd Squadron (Portland), FPS
(Rosyth), 10th Squadron (RNR).

Fleet Air Arm

Aircraft	Role	Deployment	No. of sqdns or flights
Buccaneer 2	Strike	Carrier	1 Sqdn
Gannet 3	AEW	Carrier	1 Flight
Gannet 3	AEW	Lossiemouth	1Sqdn
Phantom FG1	FGA	Carrier	1 Sqdn

Helicopters

Lynx	Aircrew Training	Yeovilton	1 Sqdn
Lynx	ASW	Destroyers and Frigates	4 Flights
Sea King	ASW	Carrier	1 Sqdn
Sea King	ASW	ASW Carrier	1 Sqdn
Sea King	ASW	Cruisers	2 Sqdns
Sea King	ASW	Prestwick	1 Sqdn
Sea King	Aircrew Training	Culdrose	1 Sqdn
Sea King	ASW	RFAs	2 Flights
Wasp	ASW	'Leander' Class	
Wasp	ASW	'Rothesay' Class	
Wasp	ASW	'Tribal' Class	35 Flights
Wasp	ASW	Type 21	
Wasp	ASW	Type 42	
Wasp	Aircrew Training	Portland	1 Sqdn
Wessex 3	ASW	'County' Class	7 Flights
Wessex 3	Aircrew Training	Portland	1 Sqdn
Wessex 5	Commando Assault	Yeovilton/HMS *Hermes*	2 Sqdns
Wessex 5	Aircrew Training	Yeovilton	1 Sqdn
Wessex 5	Fleet Requirements	Portland	1 Sqdn

List of Pennant Numbers

Note: Not displayed on Submarines or RMAS craft.

Aircraft Carriers

R	08	Bulwark
R	09	Ark Royal
R	12	Hermes

Submarines

S	01	Porpoise
S	05	Finwhale
S	07	Sealion
S	08	Walrus
S	09	Oberon
S	10	Odin
S	11	Orpheus
S	12	Olympus
S	13	Osiris
S	14	Onslaught
S	15	Otter
S	16	Oracle
S	17	Ocelot
S	18	Otus
S	19	Opossum
S	20	Opportune
S	21	Onyx
S	22	Resolution
S	23	Repulse
S	26	Renown
S	27	Revenge
S	46	Churchill
S	48	Conqueror
S	50	Courageous
S	101	Dreadnought
S	102	Valiant
S	103	Warspite
S	104	Sceptre
S	108	Sovereign
S	109	Superb
S	111	Spartan
S	112	Severn
S	126	Swiftsure

Anti-Submarine Cruisers

CAH	1	Invincible
CAH	2	Illustrious

Cruisers

C	20	Tiger
C	99	Blake

Light Cruisers and Drestroyers

D	02	Devonshire
D	12	Kent
D	16	London
D	18	Antrim
D	19	Glamorgan
D	20	Fife
D	21	Norfolk
D	23	Bristol
D	80	Sheffield
D	86	Birmingham
D	87	Newcastle
D	88	Glasgow
D	108	Cardiff
D	118	Coventry
D	—	Exeter
D	—	Southampton

Frigates

F	10	Aurora
F	12	Achilles
F	15	Euryalus
F	16	Diomede
F	18	Galatea
F	27	Lynx
F	28	Cleopatra
F	32	Salisbury
F	38	Arethusa
F	39	Naiad
F	40	Sirius
F	42	Phoebe
F	43	Torquay
F	45	Minerva
F	47	Danae
F	52	Juno
F	54	Hardy
F	56	Argonaut
F	57	Andromeda
F	58	Hermione
F	60	Jupiter
F	69	Bacchante
F	70	Apollo
F	71	Scylla
F	72	Ariadne
F	75	Charybdis
F	88	Broadsword
F	—	Battleaxe
F	—	Brilliant
F	99	Lincoln
F	101	Yarmouth
F	103	Lowestoft
F	104	Dido
F	106	Brighton
F	107	Rothesay
F	108	Londonderry
F	109	Leander
F	113	Falmouth
F	114	Ajax
F	115	Berwick
F	117	Ashanti
F	119	Eskimo
F	122	Gurkha
F	124	Zulu
F	125	Mohawk
F	126	Plymouth
F	127	Penelope
F	129	Rhyl
F	131	Nubian
F	133	Tartar

F	169	Amazon
F	170	Antelope
F	171	Active
F	172	Ambuscade
F	173	Arrow
F	174	Alacrity
F	184	Ardent
F	185	Avenger

Assault Ships

L	10	Fearless
L	11	Intrepid

Logistic Landing Ships and LCTs

L 700-711		LCM 9
L	3004	Sir Bedivere
L	3005	Sir Galahad
L	3027	Sir Geraint
L	3029	Sir Lancelot
L	3036	Sir Percivale
L	3505	Sir Tristram
L 3507-8		LCM 9
L	3513	Empire Gull
L	4001	Ardennes
L	4002	Agheila
L	4041	Abbeville
L	4061	Audemer
L	—	Arakan
L	7037	
L	7100	

LCMs (RCT)

RPL	01	Avon
RPL	02	Bude
RPL	03	Clyde
RPL	04	Dart
RPL	05	Eden
RPL	06	Forth
RPL	07	Glen
RPL	08	Hamble
RPL	10	Kennet
RPL	11	Loddon
RPL	12	Medway

LCP

LCP	501	LCP L 3
LCP	503	LCP L 3
LCP	503	LCP L 3

LCVP

LCVP	102	LCVP 1
LCVP	112	LCVP 1
LCVP	118	LCVP 1
LCVP	120	LCVP 1
LCVP	123	LCVP 1
LCVP	127-128	LCVP 1
LCVP	134	LCVP 1
LCVP	136	LCVP 1
LCVP	142-149	LCVP 2
LCVP	150-158	LCVP 3

Helicopter Support Ship

K	08	Engadine

Minelayer

N	21	Abdiel

Support Ships and Auxiliaries

A	00	Britannia
A	70	Echo
A	71	Enterprise
A	71	Egeria
A	75	Tidespring
A	76	Tidepool
A	77	Pearleaf
A	78	Plumleaf
A	80	Orangeleaf
A	82	Cherryleaf
A	85	Faithful
A	86	Forceful
A	87	Favourite
A	88	Agile
A	89	Advice
A	90	Accord
A	93	Dexterous
A	94	Director
A	95	Typhoon
A	99	Beaulieu
A	100	Beddgelert
A	101	Bembridge
A	102	Airedale
A	103	Bibury
A	104	Blakeney
A	105	Brodick
A	106	Alsatian
A	108	Triumph
A	111	Cyclone
A	113	Alice
A	116	Agatha
A	117	Audrey
A	121	Agnes
A	122	Olwen
A	123	Olna
A	124	Olmeda
A	126	Cairn
A	127	Torrent
A	128	Torrid
A	129	Dalmatian
A	133	Hecla
A	134	Rame Head
A	137	Hecate
A	138	Herald
A	144	Hydra
A	145	Daisy
A	155	Deerhound
A	162	Elkhound
A	168	Labrador
A	169	Husky
A	171	Endurance
A	177	Edith
A	179	Whimbrel

A	180	Mastiff
A	182	Saluki
A	187	Forth
A	187	Sealyham
A	188	Pointer
A	189	Setter
A	191	Berry Head
A	201	Spaniel
A	210	Charlotte
A	217	Christine
A	218	Clare
A	220	Loyal Moderator
A	222	Spapool
A	231	Reclaim
A	232	Kingarth
A	236	Wakeful
A	250	Sheepdog
A	252	Doris
A	259	St. Margarets
A	261	Eddyfirth
A	268	Green Rover
A	269	Grey Rover
A	270	Blue Rover
A	271	Gold Rover
A	273	Black Rover
A	274	Ettrick
A	277	Elsing
A	280	Resurgent
A	281	Kinbrace
A	288	Sea Giant
A	289	Confiance
A	290	Confident
A	310	Invergordon
A	317	Bulldog
A	319	Beagle
A	320	Fox
A	322	Bridget
A	323	Betty
A	324	Barbara
A	325	Fawn
A	327	Basset
A	328	Collie
A	329	Retainer
A	330	Corgi
A	332	Caldy
A	334	Bern
A	335	Brenda
A	336	Lundy
A	338	Skomer
A	339	Lyness
A	340	Graemsay
A	344	Stromness
A	345	Tarbatness
A	346	Switha
A	338	Epworth
A	353	Elkstone
A	354	Froxfield
A	361	Roysterer
A	364	Whitehead
A	367	Newton

A	377	Maxim
A	378	Kinterbury
A	379	Throsk
A	382	Vigilant (ex-*Loyal Factor*)
A	384	Felsted
A	385	Fort Grange
A	386	Fort Austin
A	389	Clovelly
A	393	Dunster
A	394	Foxhound
A	404	Bacchus
A	406	Hebe
A	480	Resource
A	482	Kinloss
A	486	Regent
A	502	Rollicker
A	507	Uplifter
A	510	Alert (ex-*Loyal Governor*)
A	1771	Loyal Proctor
A	1772	Holmwood
A	1773	Horning

Auxiliaries

RDV	01	Crystal

Auxiliaries

Y	15	Watercourse
Y	16	Waterfowl
Y	17	Waterfall
Y	18	Watershed
Y	19	Waterspout
Y	20	Waterside
Y	21	Oilpress
Y	22	Oilstone
Y	23	Oilwell
Y	24	Oilfield
Y	25	Oilbird
Y	26	Oilman

Boom Defence Vessels

P	190	Laymoor
P	191	Layburn
P	192	Mandarin
P	193	Pintail
P	194	Garganey
P	195	Goldeneye
P	196	Goosander
P	197	Pochard

Light Forces

P	260	Kingfisher
P	261	Cygnet
P	262	Petrel
P	263	Sandpiper
P	271	Scimitar
P	274	Cutlass
P	275	Sabre
P	276	Tenacity
P	295	Jersey
P	297	Guernsey

P	298	Shetland
P	299	Orkney
P	300	Lindisfarne
P	1007	Beachampton
P	1055	Monkton
P	1089	Wasperton
P	1093	Wolverton
P	1096	Yarnton
P	3104	Dee (ex-*Beckford*)
P	3113	Droxford

Coastal Minesweepers

M	29	Brecon
M	1103	Alfriston
M	1109	Bickington
M	1110	Bildeston
M	1113	Brereton
M	1114	Brinton
M	1115	Bronington
M	1116	Wilton
M	1124	Crichton
M	1125	Cuxton
M	1133	Bossington
M	1140	Gavington
M	1141	Glasserton
M	1146	Hodgeston
M	1147	Hubberston
M	1151	Iveston
M	1153	Kedleston
M	1154	Kellington
M	1157	Kirkliston
M	1158	Laleston
M	1165	Maxton
M	1166	Nurton
M	1167	Repton
M	1173	Pollington
M	1180	Shavington
M	1181	Sheraton
M	1182	Shoulton
M	1187	Upton
M	1188	Walkerton
M	1195	Wotton
M	1200	Soberton
M	1204	Stubbington
M	1208	Lewiston
M	1216	Crofton

Inshore Minesweepers

M	2002	Aveley
M	2010	Isis (ex-*Cradley*)
M	2614	Bucklesham TRV
M	2621	Dittisham
M	2622	Downham TRV
M	2626	Everingham TRV
M	2628	Flintham
M	2630	Fritham TRV
M	2635	Haversham TRV
M	2636	Lasham TRV
M	2716	Pagham RNXS
M	2717	Fordham DGV

M	2720	Waterwitch (ex-*Powderham*)
M	2726	Shipham RNXS
M	2733	Thakeham RNXS
M	2735	Tongham RNXS
M	2737	Warmingham DGV
M	2780	Woodlark (ex-*Yaxham*)
M	2781	Portisham RNXS
M	2784	Puttenham RNXS
M	2790	Thatcham DGV
M	2793	Thornham

DGV	=	*Degaussing Vessels*
RNXS	=	*Royal Naval Auxiliary Service*
TRV	=	*Torpedo Recovery Vessels*
R	=	Reserve (ex-RAF)

Ark Royal

Aircraft Carriers

Type: Aircraft Carrier

Class: "Ark Royal"

Name	No.	Builders	Laid down	Launched	Commissioned
ARK ROYAL	R 09	Cammell Laird & Co Ltd, Birkenhead	3 May 1943	3 May 1950	25 Feb 1955

Displacement, tons: 43,060; 50,786 full load

Length, feet (metres): 720.0 (219.5) pp; 845.0 (257.6) oa

Beam, feet (metres): 112.8 (34.4) hull

Draught, feet (metres): 36.0 (11.0)

Width, feet (metres): 168.0 (51.2)

Catapults: 2 improved steam

Aircraft: 30 fixed wing + 9 helicopters

Armour: 4.5 in belt; 4 in flight deck; 2.5 in hangar deck; 1.5 in hangar side

Main engines: Parsons single reduction

geared turbines; 4 shafts; 152,000 shp

Boilers: 8 Admiralty 3-drum type; pressure 400 psi (28.1 kg/cm²); superheat 600°F (316°C)

Speed, knots: 31.5

Oil fuel, tons: 5,500 capacity

Complement: 260 officers (as Flagship); 2,380 ratings (with Air Staff)

The experience of the early years of World War II was grafted into the design of the new ships of what became the "Ark Royal" class.

These were to be the largest aircraft carriers built for the Royal Navy and four were originally planned – *Irresistible*, *Audacious*, *Africa* and *Eagle*. The last two were cancelled and the first two renamed *Ark Royal* after her predecessor was sunk in

November 1941 and *Eagle*, whose forerunner was sunk in August 1942. A further series of cancellations removed an even larger class of carriers – *Gibraltar*, *Malta* and *New Zealand* – from the plan. *Eagle* (ex-*Audacious*) was laid down in

October 1942 to be followed six months later by *Ark Royal* (ex-*Irresistible*). The war was over before *Eagle* was launched in March 1946 and, completed in October 1951, her service career at sea was to end in 1972 when she was paid off into reserve at Plymouth.

Ark Royal's launch was not until May 1950 but her completion was delayed largely as the result of a meeting at Bedford in August 1951. It was here that Captain D.R.F. Campbell produced his original suggestion for an angled deck to do away with the danger of barrier accidents which then existed. In 1952 touch-and-go landings were made on *Triumph* and USS *Midway* with the angled area painted on the flight deck. By December of that year the USN had converted USS *Antietam* for an 8° angled deck and its success caused the delay in *Ark Royal's* completion. By the time she commissioned in February 1955 she had been fitted with a 5.5° angled deck and an extra lift on the port deck-edge. In addition two other British inventions, the mirror landing sight and a pair of steam catapults, were incorporated and her trials, from June 1954 to February 1955, proved to her new captain, Captain D.R.F. Campbell, that this ship was a great advance on her predecessors.

The Defence White Paper of 1958 allowed for four carriers in service of which one was to be *Ark Royal*. The steady progression of aircraft design provided the Sea Venom and the Scimitar but in 1962 the first squadron of Buccaneers joined *Ark Royal*. This was the most advanced fixed-wing carrier aircraft designed in Britain and was to give excellent service. The following year *Ark Royal* carried out the first carrier landings in the RN of a V/STOL aircraft, the Hawker P1127, the predecessor of the Harrier – three years before a similar test by the USN. It was to be thirteen years before the Government approved a small programme of the latter aircraft.

In 1966 the Defence White Paper had demolished any chance of the Royal Navy maintaining an aircraft-carrier element but in March 1967 *Ark Royal* started a special refit and modernisation to allow her to operate Phantom and Buccaneer aircraft. This involved the extension of the angled deck to 8.5°, an increase in the sizes of the flight-deck and island and the fitting of a powerful waist catapult and improved arresting gear. She came out of the yard in February 1970, her refit having cost £32,500,000. At this time she had a maximum of eight years life ahead of her. The cost was probably not unreasonable considering that *Eagle's* reconstruction in 1959-64 had cost £31,000,000, although the impossibility of comparing figures is shown by *Ark Royal's* original building cost of £21,428,000.

Thus the *Ark Royal* has undergone a series of major modifications throughout her long and busy life. Too late for the Korean War and in refit at the time of Suez she has steamed many thousands of miles in carrying out present day naval duties and will go into reserve in December 1978 in place of *Eagle*, with *Hermes* and *Bulwark* taking the bulk of the weight until *Invincible* commissions in 1979-80. But with her will pass the necessary and honourable era of the fixed-wing aircraft carrier in the Royal Navy.

Ark Royal

Type: Helicopter/VSTOL Carrier

Class: "Hermes"

Name	No.	Builders	Laid down	Launched	Commissioned
HERMES	R 12	Vickers (Shipbuilding) Ltd, Barrow-in-Furness	21 June 1944	16 Feb 1953	18 Nov 1959

Displacement, tons: 23,900 standard; 28,700 full load
Length, feet (metres): 650.0 (198.1) pp; 744.3 (226.9) oa
Beam, feet (metres): 90.0 (27.4) hull
Draught, feet (metres): 28.5 (9.0)
Width, feet (metres): 160.0 (48.8) oa
Aircraft: A squadron of Sea King and Wessex 5 helicopters
Armour: Reinforced flight deck (0.75 in) – 1.2 in over magazines and machinery spaces
Missiles: 2 quadruple Seacat launchers either side abaft the after lift
Main engines: Parsons geared turbines; 2 shafts; 76,000 shp

Boilers: 4 Admiralty 3-drum type
Speed, knots: 28
Oil fuel, tons: 4,200 furnace; 320 diesel
Complement: 1,350 (143 officers, 1,207 ratings). In emergency a Commando can be embarked.

In 1945 a re-appraisal of future aircraft-carrier needs resulted in the cancellation not only of five large fleet carriers but also of four 18,300 ton light fleet carriers of which one was to be called *Hermes*. This was to be the tenth ship of the name, her immediate predecessor being the aircraft-carrier sunk by the Japanese off Ceylon in April 1942.

But the name was revived for the fourth of the four survivors of this class which were originally *Albion, Centaur, Bulwark* and *Elephant.* Although the name of the last of these was of greater antiquity than *Hermes* recent associations caused it to be changed. Despite the fact that she was laid down in June 1944 it was nearly nine years before she was launched and another six and a half years before commissioning. But in these fifteen years many things had happened to *Hermes'* design – in the finishing-school of Fleet Air Arm thought she had outstripped her sisters. She joined the fleet complete with angled deck, deck-edge lift, mirror landing sight, steam catapult and

3D radar – a thoroughly up-to-date fixed-wing carrier, although her speed of twenty-eight knots reduced her overall capability in company and she could carry no more than twenty fixed-wing aircraft and eight helicopters.

With the 1966 decision to delete aircraft-carriers from the Royal Navy it was, therefore, not surprising that in 1971 *Hermes* began a conversion to Commando Ship. What was a sad commentary was that in 1966 she had completed a two year long refit for fixed-wing operations at a cost of £10,000,000. But the die was cast and after two and a half years in dockyard hands at a cost of further £25,000,000 she emerged in August 1973 with her fixed-wing capabilities, such as catapults and arrester gear, removed but with a flight-deck strengthening to accept Harriers. This bit of forward-thinking pre-dated by some five

years the Government's decision to provide that type of aircraft for the navy. She thus became the third Commando Ship in the Royal Navy, her semi-sisters *Albion* and *Bulwark* having preceded her by some ten to twelve years, the tonnage of the whole class having risen to over 23,000 tons standard. All were designed to carry a full Commando of 750 with guns and vehicles providing both helicopter and sea lift for the Royal Marines.

In 1976 came another change of role. The Government's cuts in defence spending would have resulted in a notable reduction in NATO's anti-submarine capability had not pressure, particularly from other NATO countries, caused a new approach. *Hermes* once more entered the dockyard and in January 1977 emerged as a specialised anti-submarine helicopter carrier. How long she will be allowed to survive is a matter for

the politicians although the July 1977 report by Labour's left-wing "Study Group" shows the opposition of that sector to the continuation of such ships. At the moment the first squadron of Harriers is due to embark in *Hermes* in 1980 and, presumably, the remainder of her life is governed by the length of time it takes to build the "Invincible" class of helicopter cruisers. With the experience of the last five years any forecast of this period would be foolhardy.

Hermes

Type: Helicopter VSTOL Carrier   **Class:** "Bulwark"

Name	No.	Builders	Laid down	Launched	Commissioned
BULWARK	R 08	Harland & Wolff Ltd, Belfast	10 May 1945	22 June 1948	4 Nov 1954

Displacement, tons: 23,300 standard; 27,705 full load
Length, feet (metres): 650 (198.1) pp; 737.8 (224.9) oa
Beam, feet (metres): 90 (27.4) hull
Draught, feet (metres): 28 (8.5)
Width, feet (metres): 123.5 (37.7) oa
Aircraft: 20 Wessex and Sioux Helicopters
Landing craft: 4 LCVP
Guns: 8 × 40 mm (twins) Bofors Mk V
Main engines: Parsons geared turbines; 76,000 shp; 2 shafts
Boilers: 4 Admiralty 3 drum
Speed, knots: 28
Oil fuel, tons: 3,880 furnace; 320 diesel
Complement: 980 plus 750 Royal Marine Commando and troops

The fourth of her name to be commissioned, it seemed, in 1945, that she might suffer the same fate as two of her predecessors and be cancelled before completion. But she was one of the four of her class of eight light fleet carriers to evade the knife and was launched in Belfast three years after being laid down in mid-1945. Completion was slowed down as the future shape of the Royal Navy came under review and it was not until November 1954 that she finally commissioned.

Two years later she, with her sister *Albion*, joined *Eagle* and the French carriers *Arromanches* and *La Fayette* in the Suez task force. At this time she was operating thirty Seahawks, two Avengers and a couple of Dragonfly helicopters which, in 1956, was a fair load. Two other carriers, *Ocean* and *Theseus,* were also involved in this brief

incident but their role was very different. With three types of helicopter embarked – Army Whirlwinds to carry five men, Navy Whirlwinds seven and Sycamores three – they operated twenty-two aircraft. In the first hour and a half four hundred and fifteen marines with all their heavy equipment were landed – no mean achievement from two ships which were on training duties a few weeks earlier.

This action had a direct bearing on *Bulwark's* future because, with the lesson of Suez to guide, she was put into Portsmouth Dockyard in January 1959 and left a year later after conversion to a specialised Commando Ship. This involved the removal of catapults and arrester gear as well as an increase in mess-deck capacity, alterations to below-deck stores and the fitting of davits

Bulwark ▽△

for four LCVPs. Her aircraft complement was changed to sixteen Whirlwind helicopters and her ship's company reduced from 1,100 to 980 although an additional 750 men of the Commando could be carried. Between February 1961 and August 1962 her sister *Albion* was similarly refitted although to a higher standard as dictated by lessons learned in her predecessor. These changes included additional accommodation and better aircraft facilities allowing Wessex helicopters to replace the Whirlwinds. Similar alterations were made to *Bulwark* in her 1963 refit so that her present capacity is twenty Wessex and Sioux helicopters. At the same time her complement was increased to 1,035 but her troop lift was also augmented to 900.

The ability of *Bulwark* to be at instant readiness was put to the test on several occasions, none more impressive than when during the confrontation period with Indonesia in 1966, the ship embarked the whole commando, aircraft and stores from ashore in Singapore and was under way in less than four hours. However with Britain's withdrawal of her navy from overseas the role of this type of ship came into question and *Bulwark* barely escaped the disposal list, being placed in reserve as a helicopter carrier with an A/S capability in April 1976.

With the paying off of *Ark Royal* in December 1978 *Bulwark* is to be re-activated to fill, with *Hermes,* the gap caused by delays in the "Invincible" class.

Type: Anti-Submarine Cruiser   *Class:* "Invincible"

Name	No.	Builders	Laid down	Launched	Commissioned
INVINCIBLE	CAH 1	Vickers (Shipbuilding) Ltd, Barrow-in-Furness	20 July 1973	3 May 1977	? 1979
ILLUSTRIOUS	CAH 2	Swan Hunter Ltd, Wallsend	7 Oct 1976	—	? 1980

Displacement, tons: 16,000 standard; 19,500 full load
Length, feet (metres): 632 (192.9) pp; 677 (206.6) oa
Beam, feet (metres): 90 (27.5) wl; 104.6 (31.9) deck
Draught, feet (metres): 24 (7.3)
Flight deck length, feet (metres): 550 (167.8)
Aircraft: Total of 15: 10 Sea King helicopters (also to carry 5 Harriers)
Missile launchers: Twin Sea Dart
Main engines: 4 "Olympus" gas turbines; 112,000 shp; 2 shafts (reversible gearbox)
Speed, knots: 28
Range, miles: 5,000 at 18 knots
Complement: 900l(31 officers, 265 senior ratings, 604 junior ratings) (excluding aircrew)

The idea of a through-deck had not been confined to large aircraft-carriers – ships of about 6,000 tons had been so fitted although this size did not allow for much in the way of hangars and lifts. It was not surprising, therefore, that, as the road became more rocky for the Royal Navy's planned CVA01, a design was suggested in 1962 which combined a much smaller hull with a flat top. This remained in limbo while the arguments for Britain's replacement carriers were exchanged in Whitehall. The 1966 decision to do away with this type of ship and the RAF's fallacious claim to be able to provide necessary air support to the fleet at sea missed two important points – the helicopter is a vital part of the process of anti-submarine warfare and ships of considerable size are needed to carry a

sufficient number to provide an effective force. So, after years of argument, the idea of a "through-deck cruiser" was resurrected and the order for the first of a new class was given to Vickers on 17 April 1973. She was to be named *Invincible*.

The need for a custom-built ship for this task had been shown by the conversion of the two "Tiger" class cruisers which, at an overall cost of £19,000,000, got only eight helicopters to sea between them. But with the order for *Invincible* came the problems – alterations in design invariably cause delays but in this case the whole situation was compounded by problems of shipyard manning. By mid-1975 she was a year and a half behind schedule and it now seems unlikely that she will be in full commission until 1980.

Invincible

In May 1975 the Government decided to proceed with the maritime version of the Harrier VSTOL aircraft stating that they were essential for defence at sea, a very different approach from that of a year earlier when they were described as "a very valuable additional capability". Whatever the reasoning, *Invincible* is to carry Harriers, making a much more sensible weapon system out of what will undoubtedly be a very expensive ship.

Shortly after the time of first ordering it was announced that three of the class would be ordered and the Ministry of Defence wanted all to be built at the same yard – Vickers, Barrow. In July 1975 a change took place and MoD transferred the second order to Swan Hunter with the result that an extra year would probably be added to her building time. This ship is to be named *Illustrious*.

No further news has been released about the order for the third ship (other than "it is planned") but, if any proper use is to be made of this class on a continuing basis and the current expenditure justified, a third hull is essential. With only two in service there could be times, despite immaculate planning, when the requirements of refits and maintenance could result in neither being at sea.

Invincible

Cruisers

Type: Helicopter Cruiser

Class: "Tiger"

Name	No.	Builders	Laid down	Launched	Commissioned
TIGER (ex-*Bellerophon*)	C 20	John Brown Ltd, Clydebank	1 Oct 1941	25 Oct 1945	18 Mar 1959
BLAKE (ex-*Tiger*, ex-*Blake*)	C 99	Fairfield SB & Eng. Govan	17 Aug 1942	20 Dec 1945	8 Mar 1961

Displacement, tons: 9,500 standard; 12,080 full load
Length, feet (metres): 538.0 (164.0) pp; 550.0 (167.6) wl; 566.5 (172.8) oa
Beam, feet (metres): 64.0 (19.5)
Draught, feet (metres): 23.0 (7.0)
Aircraft: 4 Sea King helicopters
Missile launchers: 2 quadruple Seacat
Guns: 2 × 6-in (152 mm) (1 twin); 2 × 3-in (76 mm) (twin)

Armour: Belt 3.5 in × 3.2 in (89 × 83 mm); deck 2 in (51 mm); turret 3 in × 1 in (76 × 25 mm)
Main engines: 4 Parsons geared turbines; 4 shafts; 80,000 shp
Boilers: 4 Admiralty 3-drum type
Speed, knots: 30
Range, miles: 2,000 at 30 knots; 4,000 at 20 knots; 6,500 at 13 knots
Oil fuel, tons: 1,850

Complement: 85 officers, 800 ratings

In the later years of World War II there was a series of orders which, because of numerous name changes, are thoroughly confusing. Although there was some difference in design the ships concerned were all of sufficient similarity to be considered together – the following table may be of some use:

Tiger	Ordered 1942, renamed *Bellerophon,* renamed *Blake,* renamed *Bellerophon,* cancelled March 1946
Hawke	Cancelled March 1946
Centurion	Cancelled March 1946
Edgar	Cancelled March 1946
Mars	Cancelled March 1946
Neptune	Cancelled March 1946
Defence	Laid down June 1942, renamed *Lion* October 1957, completed July 1960
Bellerophon	Laid down October 1941, renamed *Tiger* February 1945, completed March 1959
Blake	Laid down August 1942, renamed *Tiger* December 1944, renamed *Blake* February 1945, completed March 1961

The three survivors of these nine ships were originally designed to mount nine 6-inch guns and ten 4-inch guns and to carry out the multifarious duties associated with cruisers over many years. In July 1946 work on them was stopped, leaving Fairfields, Scotts and John Browns with a gummed-up berth apiece, all the ships having been launched in 1944-45. On 15 October 1954 the Admiralty announced that work was to proceed on all three. But a new design had been prepared by this time which included a totally changed armament of four 6-inch guns of a new fully-automatic design with a 20 rpm rate of fire and six 3-inch guns in three twin turrets. The latter had a rate of fire of 120 rpm but neither system was without its snags; in fact these were the last guns of either calibre to be mounted in the Royal Navy.

As a result of the re-design of these ships it was between eighteen and nineteen years between launching and completion and none had been in commission very long before the Royal Navy's trauma over the deletion of aircraft carriers struck. Before the White Paper had been published in 1966 *Blake* was already in Portsmouth Dockyard for a conversion which, at the cost of £5,500,000 was to allow her to carry four helicopters. In 1968 *Tiger* was taken in hand by Devonport Dockyard for another four-year conversion which was to cost £13,250,000. Whether these huge sums deterred the Government or not *Lion* was not converted and was finally paid off and sent for scrap in April 1975.

The history of these ships shows two periods of importance to the Navy – the first of indecision as the Empire was progressively dissolved and the second of fallacious reasoning when the Royal Navy was divested by the Treasury of the organic air-support which is vital to its operation and which can be provided from nowhere else.

Tiger

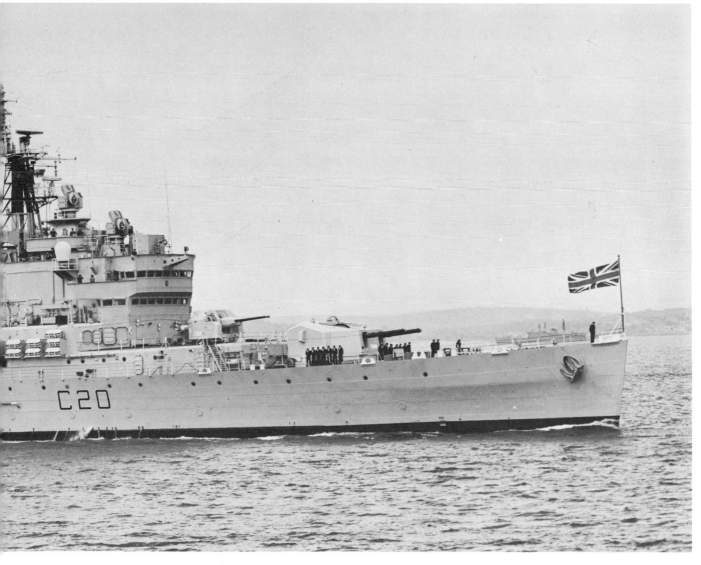

Light Cruisers

Type: Light Cruiser   **Class:** "Bristol Type 82"

Name	No.	Builders	Laid down	Launched	Commissioned
BRISTOL	D 23	Swan Hunter Ltd.	15 Nov 1967	30 June 1969	31 Mar 1973

Displacement, tons: 6,100 standard; 7,100 full load
Length, feet (metres): 490.0 (149.4) wl; 507.0 (154.5) oa
Beam, feet (metres): 55.0 (16.8)
Draught, feet (metres): 16.8 (5.2)
Aircraft: Landing platform for 1 Wasp helicopter
Missile launchers: 1 twin Sea Dart GWS 30 launcher aft
A/S weapons: 1 Ikara single launcher forward; 1 Limbo three-barrelled mortar (Mark 10) aft
Gun: 1 × 4.5-in (115 mm) Mark 8 forward; 2 × 20 mm
Main engines: COSAG arrangement (combined steam and gas turbines) 2 sets Standard Range geared steam turbines, 30,000 shp; 2 Bristol-Siddeley marine "Olympus" TMIA gas turbines, 30,000 shp; 2 shafts

Boilers: 2
Speed, knots: 30
Fuel, tons: 900
Range, miles: 5,000 at 18 knots
Complement: 407 (29 officers, 378 ratings)

The single ship of this class is the survivor of a larger class designed to act as escorts for the new generation of aircraft-carriers (CVA01 and sisters). Two things prevented any further construction beyond the lead ship – the cancellation of CVA01 and the high cost of *Bristol* (approximately £27,000,000 overall). Although she was not laid down until over a year and a half after the 1966 White Paper foreshadowed the end of carriers the long-lead items must have been ordered well in advance and to chop her construction would have meant extra unemployment on Tyneside, a particularly sensitive political area.

Bristol started her trials on 10 April 1972 and has never been a really cost-effective investment for MoD (Navy). Although she has a reasonable on-board anti-submarine system she does not carry her own helicopter. Although her Sea Dart missile system has a surface-to-surface capability her single 4.5-inch gun allows for no errors or malfunctions in the event of a situation where missiles would be out-of-place. Up to her current (1978) refit she was also deficient in ESM and jammers, lacking the Knebworth Corvus launchers fitted in so many other ships. All in all she is a big ship with a big ship's company deprived of her primary role by governmental decision. Despite these criticisms she is a hull in a fleet desperately low in numbers and arguments for her disposal take no count of her power, seaworthiness and long range.

Type: Light Cruiser   *Class:* "County"

Name	No.	Builders	Laid down	Launched	Commissioned
DEVONSHIRE	D 02	Cammell Laird & Co Ltd, Birkenhead	9 Mar 1959	10 June 1960	15 Nov 1962
KENT	D 12	Harland & Wolff Ltd, Belfast	1 Mar 1960	27 Sept 1961	15 Aug 1963
LONDON	D 16	Swan, Hunter & Wigham Richardson, Wallsend	26 Feb 1960	7 Dec 1961	4 Nov 1963
ANTRIM	D 18	Fairfield SB & Eng Co Ltd, Govan	20 Jan 1966	19 Oct 1967	14 July 1970
GLAMORGAN*	D 19	Vickers (Shipbuilding) Ltd, Newcastle upon Tyne	13 Sept 1962	9 July 1964	11 Oct 1966
FIFE	D 20	Fairfield SB & Eng Co Ltd, Govan	1 June 1962	9 July 1964	21 June 1966
NORFOLK	D 21	Swan, Hunter & Wigham Richardson, Wallsend	15 Mar 1966	16 Nov 1967	7 Mar 1970

*Refit

Devonshire △

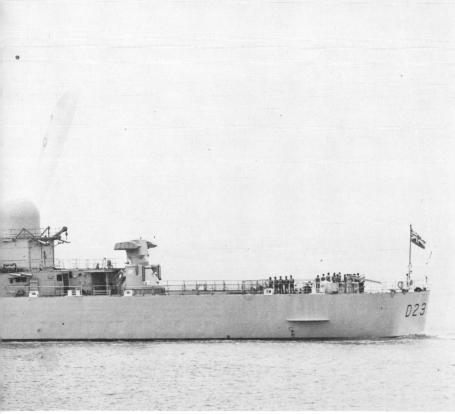

Bristol

Displacement, tons: 5,440 standard;
6,200 full load
Length, feet (metres): 505.0 (153.9) wl;
520.5 (150.7) oa
Beam, feet (metres): 54.0 (16.5)
Draught, feet (metres): 20.5 (6.3)
Aircraft: 1 Wessex helicopter
Missile launchers: 4 Exocet in four ships,
1 twin Seaslug aft;
2 quadruple Seacat either side abreast
hangar
Guns: 4 × 4.5-in (115 mm), 2 twin turrets
forward; 2 × 20-mm, (single)
(2 × 4.5-in ships with Exocet)
Main engines: Combined steam and gas
turbines, 2 sets geared steam turbines,
30,000 shp; 4 gas turbines, 30,000 shp;
2 shafts
Boilers: 2 Babcock & Wilcox
Speed, knots: 30
Complement: 471 (33 officers and 438
ratings)

There was an allowance in the 1955-56
Naval Estimates for two fleet escorts, the
first post-war design of destroyers. Instead
of being an improvement on their
predecessors of the "Daring" class they
turned out to be very much larger, the first
ships in the Royal Navy to be designed to
carry missiles. They were also the largest
ships to be propelled by a mixed steam and
gas-turbine system (COSAG) – each shaft

London △

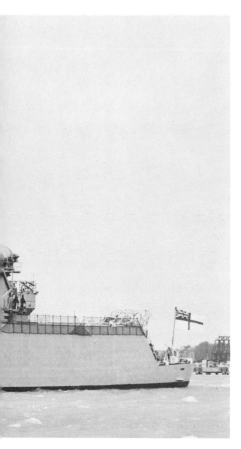

has an HP and LP steam turbine of 15,000 shp with a pair of G6 gas-turbines each of 7,500 shp. Short of full gas-turbine propulsion this was considered here as the most efficient arrangement for surface ships at the time of the first of class being laid down in 1959. It is of interest that at roughly the same time the Soviet navy was laying down the first of the all gas-turbine "Kashin" class, a revolution in naval propulsion.

The missile arrangement was a pair of "Seaslug" launchers aft and "Seacat" short range missiles abaft the after funnel. The "Seaslug" is a long-range beam-riding missile for surface-to-air operations whose development started in the early 1950s. Trials were carried out in *Girdleness* in the late 1950s and the first production models were installed in *Devonshire* and *Hampshire* in 1961-62. The pattern of action is that the surveillance radar (Type 965 or 992) detects the target and hands over control when within missile range to the heightfinder (Type 277) and the missile directing radar (Type 901). The missile itself has an HE warhead with DA and proximity fuses and a range of about 25 miles. A Mark 2 version of "Seaslug" is fitted in *Fife, Glamorgan, Antrim* and *Norfolk* of this class, a longer range version of the Mark 1 with an improved surface-to-surface capability.

The lack of a specific surface to surface system led to the introduction of the French MM 38 "Exocet" missile in the four most

modern and "Seaslug II" fitted ships. This weapon, which became operational in 1971, has a range roughly similar to "Seaslug" but is designed for anti-ship operations with a sea-skimming approach. Trial runs have proved most effective.

This class is therefore fitted for both anti-air and anti-ship operations, accepting the fact that one of the twin 4.5-inch turrets had to be removed to fit "Exocet". But, with hull-mounted sonar, the ships' only anti-submarine weapon is a single Wessex helicopter with only a limited time on task. No instant attack weapon is fitted nor do these ships carry A/S torpedo tubes. Their employment as a single unit in a submarine environment would therefore be hazardous and the lack of such weapons points the need for some system which, even if not lethal, can at least jar the nerves and deflect the purpose of the non-intrepid submariner. Some do exist.

The appearance of the various ships varies somewhat although the overall silhouette is unmistakable. *Kent* and *London* have their mainmast stepped further aft than the remainder whilst *Glamorgan, Fife, Antrim* and *Norfolk* not only have a tubular foremast and twin AKE radar aerial but are also fitted with Exocet in place of B turret.

These ships are officially rated as "destroyers" and already the first, *Hampshire*, has been paid off for disposal.

Kent

Destroyers

Name	No.	Builders	Laid down	Launched	Commissioned
SHEFFIELD	D 80	Vickers (Shipbuilding) Ltd, Barrow-in-Furness	15 Jan 1970	10 June 1971	16 Feb 1975
BIRMINGHAM	D 86	Cammell Laird & Co Ltd, Birkenhead	28 Mar 1972	30 July 1973	3 Dec 1976
NEWCASTLE	D 87	Swan Hunter Ltd, Wallsend on Tyne	21 Feb 1973	24 April 1975	23 Mar 1978
GLASGOW	D 88	Swan Hunter Ltd, Wallsend on Tyne	7 Mar 1974	14 April 1976	1978
CARDIFF	D 108	Vickers (Shipbuilding) Ltd, Barrow-in-Furness (see note)	3 Nov 1972	22 Feb 1974	1978
COVENTRY	D 118	Cammell Laird & Co Ltd, Birkenhead	22 Mar 1973	21 June 1974	1978
EXETER	—	Swan Hunter Ltd, Wallsend on Tyne	1976	—	—
SOUTHAMPTON	—	Vosper Thornycroft Ltd	21 Oct 1976	—	—
NOTTINGHAM	—	Vosper Thornycroft Ltd	—	—	—
—	—	Cammell Laird & Co Ltd, Birkenhead	—	—	—

Type: Destroyer — **Class:** "Sheffield" (Type 42)

Birmingham △▽

Displacement, tons: 3,150 standard;
4,100 full load
Length, feet (metres): 392.0 (119.5) wl;
410.0 (125.0) oa
Beam, feet (metres): 46 (14)
Draught, feet (metres): 19 (5.8)
Aircraft: 1 Lynx helicopter
Missile launchers: 1 twin Sea Dart medium
range surface-to-air (surface-to-surface
capability) GWS 30 system
Guns: 1 × 4.5-in automatic, Mark 8;
2 × 20-mm Oerlikon; 2 saluting
A/S weapons: Helicopter-launched Mk 44
torpedoes; (6 A/S torpedo tubes (triples) for
Mk 46 (except in *Sheffield*)
Main engines: COGOG arrangement of
Rolls-Royce Olympus gas turbines for full
power, 50,000 shp; 2 Rolls-Royce Tyne gas
turbines for cruising, 8,000 shp; cp
propellers; 2 shafts
Speed, knots: 30
Range, miles: 4,500 at 18 knots
Complement: 299 (26 officers, 80 senior
ratings, 193 junior ratings) accommodation
for 312

With the end of the Leander building
programme and considering the chronic
shortage of escorts for NATO operations two
new classes were put in hand. These were
the Type 42 destroyer and the Type 21
frigate.

The Type 42 is the first class of Ministry
designed British destroyers to have an all
gas-turbine propulsion system and is shorter
than might have been expected. This has
meant a more "dense" internal arrangement
calling for greater ingenuity in maintenance
and replacement of equipment. The first
ships of the class are well-spoken of for their
manoeuvrability and sea-keeping qualities
and the gas-turbines give them a very rapid
reaction time when required to get under
way or to accelerate.

Another advantage of this propulsion
system is a reduction of 25% in the
engineroom staff. The overall fall from the

471 strong ship's company of a "County"
class to 299 in the Type 42 is a very
significant saving when it is remembered
that, in general terms, half the cost of a
warship from start to finish is taken up by
her manpower. Technical courses cost a
great deal and occupy long periods – any
reduction here is most welcome.

From the weapon point-of-view some
criticism has been brought to bear on the
Type 42 for having only one twin launcher
for Sea Dart and a single 4.5-inch gun. This
criticism must be seen to be valid by anyone
who has suffered from weapon malfunctions
at critical times but, from the missile side,
the cost is very daunting and space is
limited. Since first approval in 1963 the total
for development and quantity production of
the GWS 30 (Sea Dart) system (at May 1975
prices) is in excess of £300,000,000. For this
sum, however, the Royal Navy now has a
system of considerable flexibility with a
rapid launch rate and capable of engaging
a number of targets at all altitudes as well as
surface ships.

The anti-submarine weaponry is confined
to the helicopter and A/S torpedoes, no
instant reaction weapon being fitted.
Presumably it is again lack of space that has
dictated the embarkation of only one
helicopter. Both the Canadian "Iroquois"
class and the Italian "Audace" class can
carry two helicopters but the first is 16 feet
and the second 36 feet longer than the
Type 42. Perhaps an extra 25-30 feet in the
Type 42's length could have made a
significant increase in air-capability
possible. This is even more important when
the Lynx helicopter is embarked as this
aircraft will be armed with the Sea Skua
(CK 834) air-to-surface missile for action
against fast attack craft and lightly
defended surface ships.

Although not specifically listed in the
government defence cuts the final total of
this class has undoubtedly been affected by
the reduction of one-seventh in overall

Sheffield △▽

numbers. The last three of this class was ordered on 27 May 1977 (with further orders planned) giving completion dates in the early 1980s. *Sheffield* may be distinguished from her sisters by the round vent either side of the funnel.

Two of this class *Hercules* (D28) and *Santissima Trinidad* (D29) have been built for Argentina with similar funnel to *Sheffield*.

Newcastle

Frigates

Type: Frigate				Class: "Broadsword" (Type 22)		
Name	No.	Builders	Laid down	Launched	Commissioned
BROADSWORD	F 88	Yarrow (Shipbuilders) Ltd, Glasgow	7 Feb 1975	12 May 1976	Late 1978?
BATTLEAXE	—	Yarrow (Shipbuilders) Ltd, Glasgow	1976	18 May 1977	—
BRILLIANT	—	Yarrow (Shipbuilders) Ltd, Glasgow	1977	—	—
BOXER	—	Yarrow (Shipbuilders) Ltd, Glasgow	1978	—	—

Displacement, tons: 3,500 standard; 4,000 full load
Length, feet (metres): 430 (131.2) oa
Beam, feet (metres): 48.5 (14.8)
Draught, feet (metres): 14 (4.3)
Aircraft: 2 Lynx helicopters
Missile launchers: 2 Seawolf surface-to-air systems; 4 Exocet launchers forward
Guns: 2 × 40-mm
A/S weapons: 6 (2 triple) Mk 32 torpedo tubes for Mk 44 or Mk 46; helicopters A/S torpedoes
Main engines: COGOG arrangement of 2 Rolls-Royce "Olympus" gas turbines; 56,000 bhp and 2 Rolls-Royce "Tyne" gas turbines; 8,500 bhp; 2 shafts
Speed, knots: 30 + (18 on Tynes)
Range, miles: 4,500 at 18 knots (on Tynes)
Complement: 250 (approx)

The recent designs for Royal Naval ships have set a series of "firsts" – the "Broadsword" class is the first major warship ever built in the United Kingdom without any major gun armament. This is possibly the reflection of the Government's statement that this class is intended "primarily for anti-submarine work". The basis of this capability is the new computerised Type 2016 hull-mounted sonar and, for once, the inclusion of two Lynx helicopters in the design. This has been achieved on a hull twenty feet longer than that of the Type 42 and provides a much-enhanced capability for both A/S operations and action with the anti-surface-ship Sea Skua missiles when they enter service.

Surface-to-surface armament is confined to a pair of 40-mm guns and four MM38 Exocet launchers – adequate for a peace-time patrol or, in the latter case, for countering surface threats in war. The anti-air armament is provided by two Seawolf (GWS 25) systems which are capable of engaging small Mach 2 missile and aircraft targets. In this system detection of both high- and low-angle targets is the task of the Type 967/968 radars and tracking is carried out by either Type 910 radar or television scanners. The control is of a highly complex computerised design while loading is by hand, presumably in a bid to reduce top-weight.

Steady increases in the cost of Seawolf took place between 1972 and mid-1975 of 17% for development and 12% for subsequent production. The final result, including the expected production run, was stated to be £180,000,000 at May 1975 prices, giving the Royal Navy what is probably the best point-defence missile system in the world.

It will be later than planned in its deployment at sea not primarily because of delays in the missile programme but because Type 22 orders were issued late. This, combined with yard-manning problems and certain difficulties over design and procurement, means that the Type 22s will commission some two years later than originally planned. The fifth ship was to be ordered in 1978.

Broadsword

Broadsword

Type: Frigate   *Class:* "Amazon" (Type 21)

Name	No.	Builders	Laid down	Launched	Commissioned
AMAZON	F 169	Vosper Thornycroft Ltd, Woolston	6 Nov 1969	26 April 1971	11 May 1974
ANTELOPE	F 170	Vosper Thornycroft Ltd, Woolston	23 Mar 1971	16 Mar 1972	19 July 1975
ACTIVE	F 171	Vosper Thornycroft Ltd, Woolston	23 July 1971	23 Nov 1972	17 June 1977
AMBUSCADE	F 172	Yarrow (Shipbuilders) Ltd, Glasgow	1 Sept 1971	18 Jan 1973	5 Sept 1975
ARROW	F 173	Yarrow (Shipbuilders) Ltd, Glasgow	28 Sept 1972	5 Feb 1974	29 July 1976
ALACRITY	F 174	Yarrow (Shipbuilders) Ltd, Glasgow	5 Mar 1973	18 Sept 1974	2 July 1977
ARDENT	F 184	Yarrow (Shipbuilders) Ltd, Glasgow	26 Feb 1974	9 May 1975	13 Oct 1977
AVENGER	F 185	Yarrow (Shipbuilders) Ltd, Glasgow	30 Oct 1974	20 Nov 1975	April 1978

Displacement, tons: 2,750 standard; 3,250 full load

Length, feet (metres): 360.0 (109.7) wl; 384.0 (117.0) oa

Beam, feet (metres): 41.8 (12.7)

Draught, feet (metres): 19.0 (6.8)

Aircraft: 1 Lynx helicopter

Missile launchers: 1 quadruple Seacat surface-to-air (later ships planned to have Seawolf); 2 Twin Exocet MM 38

Guns: 1 × 4.5-in Mark 8; 2 × 20-mm Oerlikon (singles)

A/S weapons: Helicopter launched torpedoes; 6 A/S torpedo tubes for Mk 46 (from F 171 onwards

Main engines: COGOG arrangement of 2 Rolls-Royce "Olympus" gas turbines 56,000 bhp; 2 Rolls-Royce "Tyne" gas turbines for cruising 8,500 shp; 2 shafts; controllable pitch, 5-bladed propellers

Speed, knots: 32; 18 on Tyne GTs

Range, miles: 3,500 at 18 knots; 1,200 at 30 knots

Complement: 179 (13 officers and 164 ratings)

One of the strengths of the Royal Navy in the early years of this century was the series of commercial designs which were produced for destroyers. Later, had it not been for the speed with which Smith's Dock Company produced the designs for the "Flower" class corvettes in 1939 and their wartime successors of the "Castle" class the escort situation would have been even worse than it was in the event. In the post-war years, however, design of major warships was centralised in the Admiralty departments at Bath and it was not until 1968 that Vosper Thornycroft were awarded a contract to plan and build a class of frigates, working in conjunction with Yarrows. The lead ship of this Type 21 was laid down in November 1969 at Woolston, the first all gas-turbine frigate to be conceived as such, pre-dating the Type 42 destroyers by three months.

When *Amazon* commissioned in May 1974 she was seen to be a most handsome ship which mounted only one major gun, had no missiles other than the close-range Seacat

and whose anti-submarine system was a single Wasp helicopter. This was not the fault of the designers – weapon capability is the responsibility of the Ministry of Defence. Within two years realisation of these deficiencies had resulted in the mounting of four MM 38 Exocet surface-to-surface missiles and plans to include six torpedo tubes for A/S torpedoes. There was no space to add to the single helicopter and the lone gun but the tradition of up-dating a ship's weapon-systems within a very short time had been adhered to. This, however, is not all bad – evaluation trials of Exocet did not start until October 1972, so reaction to their success was not too-long delayed.

Eight of this class were planned and all have at least been completed although delays have resulted from numerous changes in Ministry requirements and the failure of some sub-contractors to deliver gear on time.

Arrow

Alacrity △

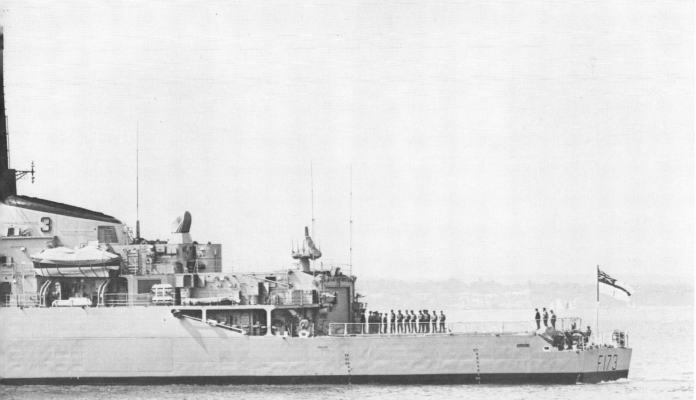

Type: Frigate | **Class:** "Broad-beamed Leander" and "Leander"

Name	No.	Builders	Laid down	Launched	Commissioned
Ikara Group					
AURORA	F 10	John Brown & Co (Clydebank) Ltd	1 June 1961	28 Nov 1962	9 April 1964
EURYALUS	F 15	Scotts Shipbuilding & Eng Co, Greenock	2 Nov 1961	6 June 1963	16 Sept 1964
GALATEA	F 18	Swan, Hunter & Wigham Richardson, Tyne	29 Dec 1961	23 May 1963	25 April 1964
ARETHUSA	F 38	J. Samuel White & Co Ltd, Cowes	7 Sept 1962	5 Nov 1963	24 Nov 1965
NAIAD	F 39	Yarrow & Co Ltd, Scotstoun, Glasgow	30 Oct 1962	4 Nov 1963	15 Mar 1965
LEANDER	F 109	Harland & Wolff Ltd, Belfast	10 April 1959	28 June 1961	27 Mar 1963
AJAX	F 114	Cammell Laird & Co Ltd, Birkenhead	12 Oct 1959	16 Aug 1962	10 Dec 1963
PENELOPE (see "Trials" note)*	F 127	Vickers-Armstrong Ltd, Tyne	14 Mar 1961	17 Aug 1962	31 Oct 1963
Exocet Group					
CLEOPATRA	F 28	HM Dockyard, Devonport	19 June 1963	25 Mar 1964	4 Jan 1966
SIRIUS	F 40	HM Dockyard, Portsmouth	9 Aug 1963	22 Sept 1964	15 June 1966
PHOEBE	F 42	Alex Stephen & Sons Ltd, Glasgow	3 June 1963	8 July 1964	15 April 1966
MINERVA*	F 45	Vickers-Armstrong Ltd, Tyne	25 July 1963	19 Dec 1964	14 May 1966
DANAE*	F 47	HM Dockyard, Devonport	16 Dec 1964	31 Oct 1965	7 Sept 1967
JUNO	F 52	John I. Thornycroft Ltd, Woolston	16 July 1964	24 Nov 1965	18 July 1967
ARGONAUT*	F 56	Hawthorn Leslie Ltd, Hebburn-on-Tyne	27 Nov 1964	8 Feb 1966	17 Aug 1967
DIDO*	F 104	Yarrow & Co Ltd, Scotstoun, Glasgow	2 Dec 1959	22 Dec 1961	18 Sept 1963
Broad-beamed Group					
ACHILLES	F 12	Yarrow & Co Ltd, Scotstoun, Glasgow	1 Dec 1967	21 Nov 1968	9 July 1970
DIOMEDE	F 16	Yarrow & Co Ltd, Scotstoun, Glasgow	30 Jan 1968	15 April 1969	2 April 1971
ANDROMEDA*	F 57	HM Dockyard, Portsmouth	25 May 1966	24 May 1967	2 Dec 1968
HERMIONE	F 58	Alex Stephen & Sons Ltd, Glasgow	6 Dec 1965	26 April 1967	11 July 1969
JUPITER	F 60	Yarrow & Co Ltd, Scotstoun, Glasgow	3 Oct 1966	4 Sept 1967	9 Aug 1969
BACCHANTE	F 69	Vickers-Armstrong Ltd, Tyne	27 Oct 1966	29 Feb 1968	17 Oct 1969
APOLLO	F 70	Yarrow & Co Ltd, Scotstoun, Glasgow	1 May 1969	15 Oct 1970	28 May 1972
SCYLLA	F 71	HM Dockyard, Devonport	17 May 1967	8 Aug 1967	12 Feb 1970
ARIADNE	F 72	Yarrow & Co Ltd, Scotstoun, Glasgow	1 Nov 1969	10 Sept 1971	10 Feb 1973
CHARYBDIS	F 75	Harland & Wolff Ltd, Belfast	27 Jan 1967	28 Feb 1968	2 June 1969

*Refit

Arethusa △

Cleopatra

Displacement, tons: 2,450 standard;
2,500 standard (broad-beamed)
2,860 full load (Ikara Group);
3,200 full load (Exocet Group)
Length, feet (metres): 360 (109.7) wl, 372
(113.4) oa
Beam, feet (metres): 41 (12.5) (Leanders);
43 (13.1) (Broad-beamed)
Draught, feet (metres): 18 (5.5);
18.5 (5.6) (Exocet Group)
Aircraft: 1 Wasp helicopter
Missiles: Ikara Group: 2 quad Seacat
Exocet Group: 1 MM 00 Exocet (forward),
3 quad Seacat (2 att, 1 forward)
Broad-beamed Group: 1 quad Seacat
Guns: Ikara Group: 2 × 40 mm
Exocet Group: 2 × 40 mm
Broad-beamed Group: 2 × 4.5 in (115 mm)
(twin); 2 × 20 mm
A/S weapons: Ikara Group: Ikara
(foreward); 1 Limbo (aft)
Exocet Group: 2 triple Mk 32 torpedo tubes
Broad-beamed Group: 1 Limbo
Main engines: 2 double reduction geared
turbines; 2 shafts; 30,000 shp
Boilers: 2
Speed, knots: 30
Oil fuel, tons: 460
Complement: 251 (Leanders);
260 (Broad-beamed)

After what can only be described as a series
of experimental classes of frigate the first of
the "Leander" class was laid down in spring
1959. She was an improvement on the
"Rothesay" class and, like the Type 81, was
designed to carry a helicopter although
Leander was provided with a hangar. She
also carried a long-range air warning radar,
the then new Seacat surface-to-air missiles
and improved sonar. The latter was planned
to operate with the helicopter, giving instant

Andromeda △

Naiad

attack capability in the event of a long-range sonar detection. This was the Match system, on which great hopes were set although it suffered from the same problems as all hull-mounted sonars.

Seven of this class were ordered in the initial stages and, finally, sixteen were built by 1967. By this time the first of ten "broad-beamed Leanders" had been laid down with an extra two feet beam to provide additional stability. There were variations, too, in the machinery fit. The first ten had Y-100 machinery, the next six Y-136 and the "broad-beamed" ships Y-160. The ultimate result from the speed point-of-view was much the same and the range unchanged.

The "Leanders" were described as "general-purpose" frigates but their design just pre-dated the introduction of missiles and long-range A/S weapons and they were long out-dated by the time the later ships were completed. This had been foreseen a number of years before but it was not until 1972 that the first conversion was at sea. This was *Leander,* who had had her 4.5-inch turret and her long-range Type 965 radar removed to allow the fitting of the Australian anti-submarine weapon system Ikara. Nearly nine years before this system had been fitted in HMAS *Stuart,* and subsequently in the remainder of the Australian "River" class, without the need for removing the gun turret. The necessity for taking out the only major gun armament of the British "Leanders" has never been satisfactorily explained.

Eight of the original class were scheduled for the Ikara conversion, the remainder being planned for an Exocet conversion. As this alteration was introduced in the two

Chilean "Leander" class with the missiles mounted well aft there was some surprise when the first British conversion, *Cleopatra,* emerged in November 1975 with her Exocet launchers mounted well forward, again replacing the 4.5-inch turret. As converted ships were provided with a gun armament of only two 40-mm guns their ability to act in support roles where artillery cover was required was nil. Presumably this was part of a governmental decision that these ships would never be used in such actions, a debatable point when their total numbers provided well over a third of the total Royal Naval destroyer and frigate force. Their recent employment has included a substantial participation in the so-called "Cod War" off Iceland where, luckily, no gunnery was required. The last of this class could well be on the active list at the turn of the 21st Century.

The first "broad-beamed Leander" to undergo a conversion including provision of four Exocet launchers, Seawolf, improved Sonar and new ECM is *Andromeda* who was taken in hand late-1977.

Several of this class serve with other navies – Chile (2), India (6), New Zealand (2) and Netherlands (6) plus the Australian "Rivers".

Euryalus

Type: Frigate   *Class:* "Tribal" (Type 81)

Name	No.	Builders	Laid down	Launched	Commissioned
ASHANTI	F 117	Yarrow & Co Ltd, Scotstoun, Glasgow	15 Jan 1958	9 Mar 1959	23 Nov 1961
ESKIMO	F 119	J. Samuel White & Co Ltd, Cowes	22 Oct 1958	20 Mar 1960	21 Feb 1963
GURKHA	F 122	J. I. Thornycroft & Co Ltd, Woolston	3 Nov 1958	11 July 1960	13 Feb 1963
ZULU	F 124	Alex Stephen & Sons Ltd, Govan	13 Dec 1960	3 July 1962	17 April 1964
MOHAWK	F 125	Vickers-Armstrong Ltd, Barrow-in-Furness	23 Dec 1960	5 April 1962	29 Nov 1963
NUBIAN	F 131	HM Dockyard, Portsmouth	7 Sept 1959	6 Sept 1960	9 Oct 1962
TARTAR*	F 133	HM Dockyard, Devonport	22 Oct 1959	19 Sept 1960	26 Feb 1962

*Refit

Nubian △

Gurkha

Displacement, tons: 2,300 standard; 2,700 full load
Length, feet (metres): 350.0 (106.7) wl; 360.0 (109.7) oa
Beam, feet (metres): 42.3 (12.9)
Draught, feet (metres): 18.0 (5.5)
Aircraft: 1 Wasp helicopter

Missile launchers: 2 quadruple Seacats
Guns: 2 × 4.5-in (singles); 2 × 20-mm
A/S weapons: 1 Limbo 3-barrelled mortar
Main engines: Combined steam and gas turbine; Metrovick steam turbine; 12,500 shp; Metrovick gas turbine; 7,500 shp; 1 shaft
Boilers: 1 Babcock & Wilcox (plus 1 auxiliary boiler)

Speed, knots: 25
Oil fuel, tons: 400
Range, miles: 4,500 at 12 knots
Complement: 253 (13 officers and 240 ratings)

The first three of this class, *Ashanti*, *Eskimo* and *Gurkha* were ordered under the 1955-56 Estimates, *Nubian* and *Tartar* those of 1956-57 and *Mohawk* and *Zulu* in 1957-58. They were thus ahead of the missile era but their propulsion system was a step ahead of their predecessors. The single shaft was driven by a combination of steam and gas turbines giving both acceleration and a swift get-away. They were designed as self-contained units for service in the Persian Gulf where manoeuvrability is frequently a necessity in coastal waters studded with coral-heads. This was not aided by the single screw which was presumably built-in to allow for cuts in costs. These were admittedly kept down to £5 6,000,000 but the unfortunate captain caught in enclosed waters with sudden gusts of high velocity has frequently wished for the turning moment of the second screw despite having twin rudders.

Two 4.5-inch guns allowed a choice in the event of malfunction and the Limbo A/S mortar was, for the first time, backed by the provision of a Wasp helicopter although there was no hangar provided. This was very much an interim class as events turned out but the first glimmerings of the modern highly automated operations room were there even though a fair part of the gear provided was antediluvian and more fitted for deep-submergence than rapid viewing.

Subsequently Seacat missiles have been fitted and, in 1970, variable-depth sonar was fitted in *Ashanti* and *Gurkha*. This class is certainly adequate for many of the duties which confront the Royal Navy today, although their speed of 25 knots is hardly up to modern anti-nuclear-submarine warfare.

Eskimo

Type: Frigate   *Class:* "Rothesay" (Modified Type 12)

Name	No.	Builders	Laid down	Launched	Commissioned
YARMOUTH	F 101	John Brown & Co Ltd, Clydebank	29 Nov 1957	23 Mar 1959	26 Mar 1960
LOWESTOFT	F 103	Alex Stephen & Sons Ltd, Govan	9 June 1958	23 June 1960	18 Oct 1961
BRIGHTON	F 106	Yarrow & Co Ltd, Scotstoun, Glasgow	23 July 1957	30 Oct 1959	28 Sept 1961
ROTHESAY*	F 107	Yarrow & Co Ltd, Scotstoun, Glasgow	6 Nov 1956	9 Dec 1957	23 April 1960
LONDONDERRY*	F 108	J. Samuel White & Co Ltd, Cowes	15 Nov 1956	20 May 1958	22 July 1960
FALMOUTH	F 113	Swan, Hunter & Wigham Richardson, Wallsend	23 Nov 1957	15 Dec 1959	25 July 1961
BERWICK	F 115	Harland & Wolff Ltd, Belfast	16 June 1958	15 Dec 1959	1 June 1961
PLYMOUTH	F 126	HM Dockyard, Devonport	1 July 1958	20 July 1959	11 May 1961
RHYL	F 129	HM Dockyard, Portsmouth	29 Jan 1958	23 April 1959	31 Oct 1960

*Refit

Displacement, tons: 2,380 standard; 2,800 full load
Length, feet (metres): 360.0 (109.7) wl; 370.0 (112.8) oa
Beam, feet (metres): 41.0 (12.5)
Draught, feet (metres): 17.3 (5.3)
Aircraft: 1 Wasp helicopter
Missile launchers: 1 quadruple Seacat
Guns: 2 × 4.5-in (115 mm) (1 twin); 2 × 20-mm (single)
A/S weapons: 1 Limbo 3-barrelled mortar
Main engines: 2 double reduction geared turbines; 2 shafts; 30,000 shp
Boilers: 2 Babcock & Wilcox
Speed, knots: 30
Oil fuel, tons: 400
Range, miles: 4,200 at 12 knots
Complement: 235 (15 officers and 220 ratings)

This class is basically similar to the earlier "Whitby" class (Type 12) with modifications resulting from experience with the latter ships which, in their turn, benefited from the Type 15 conversions of the wartime "U, V, W" and "Z" classes. In these conversions an enclosed bridge replaced the open spaces of the original design and this was continued in all future frigate construction. There were howls of dismay from some of the traditionalists but the ability to operate the ship without the distractions of rain, spray and wind were of over-riding importance, particularly in an A/S action.

The hull form of the "Whitbys" and "Rothesays" provided a steady platform and a good speed in heavy weather. Although built before the introduction of Seacat close-range missiles provision was made in the "Rothesays" for the mounting of this weapon at a later date. This in the end was 1966 when *Rothesay* was taken in hand for a two-year conversion at Rosyth. In addition to having her after 40-mm replaced by a

Rothesay ▽

quadruple Seacat she lost one of her two Limbo A/S mortars to make space for the incorporation of a flight-deck and hangar for a Wasp helicopter. This was a notable advance, greatly increasing the value of these ships. By 1972 all the class were similarly converted having internal changes built-in which consisted of a new Operations Room, a new gunnery control system and full air-conditioning.

It is interesting that the earlier ships of the Australian "River" class were of similar design although with some notable differences. The first pair (*Yarra* and *Parramatta*) had the characteristic cut-away quarter-deck which was built up in the second pair (*Stuart* and *Derwent*). The last pair (*Swan* and *Torrens*) were much more like a "Leander" but none carries a helicopter, the long-range Ikara A/S weapon being fitted instead. Two "Rothesay" class (*Otago* and *Taranaki*) serve in the RNZN.

Originally this was to be a twelve-ship class for the RN but *Weymouth*, *Hastings* and *Fowey* were re-designed as *Leander*, *Dido* and *Ajax*.

Brighton

| *Type:* Frigate | | | | | *Class:* "Whitby" (Type 12) |

Name **TORQUAY**	No. F 43	Builders Harland & Wolff Ltd, Belfast	Laid down 11 Mar 1953	Launched 1 July 1954	Commissioned 10 May 1956

Displacement, tons: 2,150 standard; 2,560 full load
Length, feet (metres): 360.0 (109.7) wl; 369.8 (112.7) oa
Beam, feet (metres): 41.0 (12.5)
Draught, feet (metres): 17 (5.2)
Guns: 2 × 4.5-in (115 mm) (twin)
A/S weapons: 1 Limbo 3-barrelled DC mortar
Main engines: 2 sets d.r. geared turbines; 2 shafts; 30,430 shp
Boilers: 2 Babcock & Wilcox; Pressure 550 psi (38.7 kg/cm²); Temperature 850°F (454°C)
Speed, knots: 31
Oil fuel, tons: 370
Complement: 225 (12 officers and 213 ratings)

The first ships of the "Whitby" class were ordered in 1951 at the same time as the "Salisbury" and "Leopard" classes. This was when an attempt was being made to provide specialised frigates to carry out the various fleet tasks – for the "Whitbys" it was anti-submarine work. At that time the new Limbo A/S mortar was being introduced after successful sea trials in the "Weapon"

class destroyer *Scorpion*. Two of these triple-barrelled mountings, which gave all-round training instead of having to point ship as was the case with the earlier "Squid", were provided in the "Whitbys". Most effective they were against the maximum dived speed of 9-10 knots expected from the average diesel boat of that period and even the 15-16 knots of the newer conversions. But *Whitby* herself commissioned eighteen months after USS *Nautilus* was first underway on nuclear power and the whole business of A/S warfare entered a new era.

But the "Whitbys" were important ships, being the first post-war British design for an A/S frigate. From the engineering stand-point they continued the advance in boiler superheat temperatures and pressures begun in the "Daring" and "Weapon" classes. Whereas the "Battle" class operated at 650°F and 400 psi, the "Weapons" at 750°F and 430 psi and the "Darings" at 850°F and 650 psi. The "Whitby's" Babcock & Wilcox boilers were designed for 850°F and 550 psi. Their turbines were double reduction geared of Y-100 design (as in the earlier "Leanders")

giving only 220 revolutions at high power. With twin rudders, good hull-form and a high propeller efficiency they achieved 30 knots at considerably lower power than was needed in earlier designs of similar displacement.

The armament was adequate for the tasks foreseen at the time of their design and originally included twelve A/S torpedo tubes (four fixed on each side with two twin trainable mountings). These were first fitted in *Scarborough* but were eventually removed and never fitted in the later ships. It is just possible that this was because no suitable weapon was available to load into the tubes.

By 1977 there were only three of this class to be seen at sea, around the UK, *Tenby*, *Scarborough* and *Whitby* having been scrapped in 1974-75. *Torquay* has been converted as a Navigational Training ship with a large deck-house aft and carries the first Computer-Assisted Action Information System (CAAIS). *Eastbourne* has been stripped of her guns and A/S armament and acts as alongside training ship for *Caledonia* at Rosyth whilst *Blackpool* (which served with the RNZN from 1966 to 1971) has been

provided with two large towers forward and was used as a shock-target in the River Forth. India has two "Whitbys" in commission, *Talwar* and *Trishul*. The former's appearance was radically changed in 1975 when her gun-turret was replaced by a pair of Soviet Styx missile-launchers, the first British-built ship to receive Russian armament.

Torquay ▽△

Type: Frigate   *Class:* "Salisbury" (Type 61)

Name	No.	Builders	Laid down	Launched	Commissioned
SALISBURY	F 32	HM Dockyard, Devonport	23 Jan 1952	25 June 1953	27 Feb 1957
LINCOLN	F 99	Fairfield SB & Eng Co Ltd, Govan	20 May 1955	6 April 1959	7 July 1960

Displacement, tons: 2,170 standard; 2,408 full load

Length, feet (metres): 320.0 (97.5) pp; 330.0 (100.6) wl; 339.8 (103.6) oa

Beam, feet (metres): 40.0 (12.2)

Draught, feet (metres): 15.5 (4.7)

Missile launchers: 1 quadruple Seacat in *Lincoln* and *Salisbury*

Guns: 2 × 4.5-in (115 mm); 1 × 40-mm (*Chichester*); 2 × 20-mm (remainder)

A/S weapons: 1 Squid triple-barrelled mortar

Main engines: 8 ASR 1 diesels in three engine rooms; 2 shafts; 14,400 bhp; 4 engines geared to each shaft

Speed, knots: 24

Oil fuel, tons: 230

Range, miles: 2,300 at full power; 7,500 at 16 knots

Complement: 237 (14 officers and 223 ratings)

These ships were of the second type of frigates ordered in 1951. Their primary task was aircraft direction for both carrier and shore-based 'planes and for this purpose were fitted with long-range surveillance radar, a heightfinder, a target indication set and a combined warning set in addition to gunnery and navigation radars. Ordinary hull-mounted sonar was linked to a Squid A/S mortar so their A/S potential was low. A twin 4.5-inch turret and a pair of 20-mm guns completed the armament.

Below decks, however, there was an important, though limiting, change. The main engines were eight Admiralty Standard Range 1 diesels in three engine rooms and coupled to two shafts through hydraulic couplings and reverse and reduction gearboxes. This arrangement produced a speed of 24 knots and an exceptionally long range adequate for convoy operations but too slow for prolonged fleet work. They were thus even more specialised than their title of "A/D frigate" suggested.

Four of the class were built and three others planned (*Exeter*, *Gloucester* and *Coventry*) but these were cancelled in 1957 in favour of three extra "Leanders". They have had a busy life throughout the world. *Chichester* was re-equipped in 1973 to act as permanent Hong-Kong guardship. This involved the removal of the Type 965 surveillance radar and the fitting of a 40-mm gun. This decision had only a brief life – in 1976 *Chichester* returned to UK after the cuts of that year's Defence Review and was placed in reserve being paid off in late-1977. *Lincoln* and *Salisbury* had meanwhile been fitted with Seacat missiles and the former was fitted with a wooden sheathing on the bow to cushion the bumps and blows of the Cod War. In December 1976 *Llandaff* was transferred to Bangladesh and became *Umar Farooq* (F16).

Lincoln

Salisbury

Type: Frigate | Class: "Leopard" (Type 41)

Name	No.	Builders	Laid down	Launched	Commissioned
LYNX	F 27	John Brown & Co Ltd, Clydebank	13 Aug 1953	12 Jan 1955	14 Mar 1957

Displacement, tons: 2,300 standard; 2,520 full load
Length, feet (metres): 320 (97.5) pp; 330 (100.6) wl; 339.8 (103.6) oa
Beam, feet (metres): 40 (12.2)
Draught, feet (metres): 16 (4.9)
Guns: 4 × 4.5-in (115 mm) (twin turrets); 1 × 40-mm
A/S weapons: 1 Squid 3-barrelled DC mortar
Main engines: 8 ASR 1 diesels in three engine rooms; 14,400 bhp; 2 shafts; 4 engines geared to each shaft
Speed, knots: 24
Oil fuel, tons: 220
Range, miles: 2,300 at full power; 7,500 at 16 knots

Complement: 235 (15 officers and 220 ratings)

In eight months of 1953 four of this class were laid down designated, "Anti-aircraft" frigates, the third of the specialised types evolved at this time. The hull and main engines were the same as their contemporaries of the "Salisbury" class and the ships were presumably intended to complement the Air Defence capabilities of that group.

Apart from the addition of an extra 4.5-inch turret the armament was similar to that of the "Salisburys" although the radar differed in having a single AKE aerial and no heightfinder. *Jaguar*, like *Lincoln* of the

Type 61, was fitted with controllable pitch propellers.

In 1963 *Lynx* was extensively re-fitted and similar work was carried out in *Jaguar* in 1966-67. All were originally intended to mount a Seacat in place of the 40-mm gun but this modification has never been carried out.

This was originally intended to be a class of five but *Panther* was transferred to India while building and renamed *Brahmaputra*. *Puma* was deleted in 1976 and *Leopard* is currently on the Disposal List. *Jaguar* was transferred to Bangladesh in July 1978 and renamed *Ali Hyder*.

Lynx

Type: Frigate | Class: "Blackwood" (Type 14)

Name	No.	Builders	Laid down	Launched	Commissioned
HARDY	F 54	Yarrow & Co Ltd, Scotstoun, Glasgow	4 Feb 1953	25 Nov 1953	12 Dec 1955

Displacement, tons: 1,180 standard; 1,456 full load
Length, feet (metres): 300 (91.4) wl; 310 (94.5) oa
Beam, feet (metres): 33.0 (10.1)
Draught, feet (metres): 11.2 (3.4) (mean)
Guns: 2 × 40-mm Bofors
A/S weapons: 2 Limbo 3-barrelled mortars
Main engines: 1 set geared turbines; 1 shaft; 15,000 shp
Boilers: 2 Babcock & Wilcox; Pressure 550 psi (38.7 kg/cm²); Temperature 850°F (454°C)

Speed, knots: 26.0
Oil fuel, tons: 275
Range, miles: 4,000 at 12 knots
Complement: 140 (8 officers and 132 ratings)

The original twelve ships of this class were laid down over a 2½-year period and designed, as their official title rather unkindly announced, to be second-rate anti-submarine frigates. For this purpose they were armed with a pair of Limbo mortars, at that time the most advanced A/S

weapon available. The original gun armament of three 40-mm guns was in accordance with their advertised role although in the early '60s one of these was removed. The third element of the armament was two pairs of 21-inch torpedo tubes mounted only in *Blackwood, Exmouth, Malcolm* and *Palliser* which were removed at about the same time as the third 40-mm.

The hull construction of this class was comparatively simple and was pre-fabricated. However in their early days in the 1st Division of the Fishery Protection

Squadron some of these ships suffered weather damage in the heavy seas encountered off Iceland. This resulted in a programme of strengthening in 1958-59.

The first of the class to be deleted was *Pellew* in 1969 followed by *Murra* in 1970, *Grafton* in 1971, *Malcolm* in 1972, *Blackwood* in 1976, with *Keppel* and *Palliser* put on the Disposal List in 1977. The current situation is that only *Hardy* remains operational with two harbour training ships – *Duncan* at Rosyth and *Russell* at Portsmouth and *Dundas* on the disposal list.

The twelfth ship of the class, *Exmouth,* was taken in hand at Chatham Dockyard for a conversion which was completed on 20 July 1968. This involved the replacement of her steam machinery by an all gas-turbine outfit – one Olympus delivering 15,000 shp and two Proteus of 6,500 shp. The arrangement of the original shafting and the use of an early version of the Olympus prevented a higher horse-power being delivered. The single shaft was fitted with a controllable-pitch propeller but, apart from an increase to 1,700 tons full load, the particulars of dimensions and armament remained the same as before. A streamlined funnel altered her appearance and in December 1976 *Exmouth* was placed in reserve and has now been paid off.

Hardy

Nuclear Powered Ballistic Missile Submarines (SSBN)

Type: Nuclear Powered Ballistic Missile Submarine (SSBN)   **Class:** "Resolution"

Name	No.	Builders	Laid down	Launched	Commissioned
RESOLUTION	S 22	Vickers (Shipbuilding) Ltd, Barrow-in-Furness	26 Feb 1964	15 Sept 1966	2 Oct 1967
REPULSE	S 23	Vickers (Shipbuilding) Ltd, Barrow-in-Furness	12 Mar 1965	4 Nov 1967	28 Sept 1968
RENOWN	S 26	Cammell Laird & Co Ltd, Birkenhead	25 June 1964	25 Feb 1967	15 Nov 1968
REVENGE	S 27	Cammell Laird & Co Ltd, Birkenhead	19 May 1965	15 Mar 1968	4 Dec 1969

*Refit

Revenge △

Renown △

Resolution

Displacement, tons: 7,500 surfaced; 8,400 dived
Length, feet (metres): 360 (109.7) pp; 425 (129.5) oa
Beam, feet (metres): 33 (10.1)
Draught, feet (metres): 30 (9.1)
Missiles, surface: 16 tubes amidships for "Polaris" A-3 SLBMs
Torpedo tubes: 6 × 21 in (533 mm) (bow)
Nuclear reactors: 1 pressurised water cooled
Main machinery: Geared steam turbines; 1 shaft
Speed, knots: 20 surfaced; 25 dived
Complement: 143 (13 officers and 130 ratings); 2 crews

In September 1955 the first ballistic missile ever fired from a submarine was launched from a Soviet "Zulu V" class. Modification of these boats for their new role took place from 1954-58 and, although their weapons were of short-range by 1978 standards, they were the first in the field. On 31 December 1957 the USN authorised the construction of their first SSBN, *George Washington,* a converted "Scorpion" class SSN. Only 2½ years later, on 20 July 1960, she fired her first two Polaris missiles off Cape Canaveral. Five years after *George Washington's* authorisation Mr Harold Macmillan, then the British Prime Minister, met President Kennedy at Nassau. This discussion of December 1962 was the culmination of two years of conferences in the Admiralty and the Cabinet and was followed by an agreement that Great Britain should build five ballistic missile

submarines, the weapons and fire control equipment to be provided by the USA, the warheads by Britain. Two years and two months design effort followed before the first of class, *Resolution,* was laid down in February 1964. In June 1967 she put to sea for the first time but, meanwhile on 15 February 1965, the fifth SSBN was cancelled by the new Labour Government. Seven years, almost to the day, after Nassau, the last of the four boats was commissioned at Birkenhead. This was six years after the first US Polaris 3 missile had been launched and ante-dated the beginning of the USN Poseidon conversion programme by ten months. At the same time the Soviet "Yankee" class SSBNs were being delivered at a rate which allowed thirty-four to commission between 1967 and 1974. In July 1969 another SSBN milestone had been reached when the first of a programme of five French boats commissioned for trials.

As in most cases of SSBN operating the "Resolution" class is manned on a two-crew basis thus allowing one crew to be transferred for leave and shore-training after a 60-day patrol. At the end of the maintenance period the second crew takes the boat on another patrol, thus ensuring maximum utilisation of these very expensive submarines.

Fleet Submarines

Type: Fleet Submarine — Class: "Trafalgar"

Name	No.	Builders	Laid down	Launched	Commissioned
TRAFALGAR	S 113	Vickers (Shipbuilding) Ltd, Barrow-in-Furness	1978	—	—

This new class is an improvement on the "Swiftsure" class in endurance, speed and equipment. First of class, *Trafalgar* SS113, ordered from Vickers (Shipbuilding) Ltd in September 1977 with a second order to be placed in 1978.

Type: Fleet Submarine (SSN) — Class: "Swiftsure'"

Name	No.	Builders	Laid down	Launched	Commissioned
SCEPTRE	S 104	Vickers (Shipbuilding) Ltd, Barrow-in-Furness	25 Oct 1973	20 Nov 1976	Mid 1978
SOVEREIGN	S 108	Vickers (Shipbuilding) Ltd, Barrow-in-Furness	17 Sept 1970	17 Feb 1973	11 July 1974
SUPERB	S 109	Vickers (Shipbuilding) Ltd, Barrow-in-Furness	16 Mar 1972	30 Nov 1974	13 Nov 1976
SPARTAN	S 111	Vickers (Shipbuilding) Ltd, Barrow-in-Furness	24 April 1976	? Dec 1978	? 1980
SPLENDID	S 112	Vickers (Shipbuilding) Ltd, Barrow-in-Furness	1 Nov 1977	? April 1980	? 1981
SWIFTSURE	S 126	Vickers (Shipbuilding) Ltd, Barrow-in-Furness	15 April 1969	7 Sept 1971	17 April 1973

Displacement, tons: 4,200 standard; 4,500 dived
Length, feet (metres): 272.0 (82.9)
Beam, feet (metres): 32.3 (9.8)
Draught, feet (metres): 27 (8.2)
Torpedo tubes: 5 × 21-in
Nuclear reactor: 1 pressurised water-cooled

Main machinery: English Electric geared steam turbines; 1 5,000 shp; 1 Paxman auxiliary diesel; 4,000 hp; 1 shaft
Speed, knots: 30 dived
Complement: 97 (12 officers and 85 men)

This is a highly-successful improvement on the previous "Valiant" design. Shorter than their predecessors and carrying one less torpedo tube they are nevertheless of higher performance and of deeper diving depth.

Sovereign visited the North Pole in 1976.

Superb

Swiftsure

Type: Fleet Submarine (SSN)　　　　　　　　　　　　　　　　　　　　　　　　*Class:* "Valiant"

Name	No.	Builders	Laid down	Launched	Commissioned
CHURCHILL	S 46	Vickers (Shipbuilding) Ltd, Barrow-in-Furness	30 June 1967	20 Dec 1968	15 July 1970
CONQUERER	S 48	Cammell Laird & Co Ltd, Birkenhead	5 Dec 1967	28 Aug 1969	9 Nov 1971
COURAGEOUS	S 50	Vickers (Shipbuilding) Ltd, Barrow-in-Furness	15 May 1968	7 Mar 1970	16 Oct 1971
VALIANT*	S 102	Vickers (Shipbuilding) Ltd, Barrow-in-Furness	22 Jan 1962	3 Dec 1963	18 July 1966
WARSPITE	S 103	Vickers (Shipbuilding) Ltd, Barrow-in-Furness	10 Dec 1963	25 Sept 1965	18 April 1967

*Refit

Displacement, tons: 3,500 standard; 4,500 dived
Length, feet (metres): 285 (86.9)
Beam, feet (metres): 33.2 (10.1)
Draught, feet (metres): 27 (8.2)
Torpedo tubes: 6 × 21-in (533 mm)
Nuclear reactor: 1 pressurised water cooled
Main machinery: English Electric Geared steam turbines; 1 shaft
Speed, knots: 28 dived
Complement: 103 (13 officers, 90 men)

The success of *Dreadnought* was sufficient to persuade the authorities to embark on an all-British design. On 31 August 1960 the placing of a contract with Vickers Ltd was announced. This was for the construction of the first of a class in which Rolls-Royce and Associates were to be responsible for the nuclear power plant and Vickers-Armstrong (Engineers) Ltd for the main machinery. The reactor was of similar design to that which had been under development at the Admiralty Reactor Test Establishment at Dounreay. The steam turbines were built by English Electric while Laurence Scott produced the main motor. So this was an all-British project and from order to commissioning took six years, a similar time-lapse from the initial order for the US Atomic Energy Commission to construct a submarine reactor to the commissioning of USS *Nautilus*.

In a number of ways this class has suffered from being the precursor of more advanced submarines but it had profound effects in many ways. At its inception the Admiralty was forced to go "all-nuclear" thus causing a radical reduction in hulls available. But the few nuclears in commission were able to nip smartly around the globe as *Valiant* herself showed when she completed a 12,000 mile dived passage from Singapore to UK in April 1967, after 28 days steaming which included exercises en route. A great deal was learned not only from such voyages but also from the submarines' participation in fleet manoeuvres, both national and NATO. The Royal Navy was forced to "think nuclear".

Valiant ▽

△ Conquerer

Type: Fleet Submarine (SSN)   *Class:* "Dreadnought"

Name	No.	Builders	Laid down	Launched	Commissioned
DREADNOUGHT	S 101	Vickers-Armstrong Ltd, Barrow-in-Furness	12 June 1959	21 Oct 1960	17 April 1963

Displacement, tons: 3,000 standard;
3,500 surfaced; 4,000 dived
Length, feet (metres): 265.8 (81.0)
Beam, feet (metres): 32.2 (9.8)
Draught, feet (metres): 26 (7.9)
Torpedo tubes: 6 × 21-in (533 mm) (bow)
Nuclear reactor: 1 S5W pressurised
water-cooled
Main machinery: Geared steam turbines;
1 shaft
Speed, knots: 28 dived
Complement: 88 (11 officers and 77 men)

The famous signal "Under way on nuclear
power" made by USS *Nautilus* on
17 January 1955 was the major turning-point
in submarine operations. The long
sought-for "true submarine" had arrived,
capable of operating underwater for months
without surfacing. Gone were the days of
anxious moves to the surface after evening
stars followed by a night of battery charging
and a dive before the dawn revealed the
submarine to her hunters. Unheard-of power
was available and higher speeds resulted.
Fresh water ceased to become a problem,
there were no external fuel tanks to rupture
and give an oil-slick for all to see and
air-conditioning was simply achieved.

The Admiralty rapidly appreciated the
importance of this development and under
the impulsive drive of Earl Mountbatten, then
First Sea Lord, and Sir Wilfred Woods who
was Flag Officer Submarines, plans were
pushed ahead to produce both the hull and
reactor for the first British nuclear
submarine. The former was successful and
the first section of the hull was placed in
position at a ceremony conducted by the
Duke of Edinburgh on 12 July 1959. But the
reactor design was much slower and the
Admiralty Station at Dounreay, Caithness
had no hope of meeting the date necessary
to marry hull to machinery. Thus Earl
Mountbatten, now Chief of Defence Staff,
organised an agreement with the USA by
which an entire propulsion plant for a USN
"Skipjack" class submarine was made
available to the RN. On 21 October 1960 HM
The Queen launched *Dreadnought* but it
was not until 1962 that the reactor and its
ancillaries were embarked, going critical
late that year. On 17 April 1963 the first
nuclear-propelled warship in the Royal Navy
was commissioned.

Problems? Of course there were problems
but these were less traumatic than might
have been expected. It was the saga of the
hair-line cracks in the hull which impressed
on all concerned the necessity for higher
standards of building than had previously
been considered adequate. Nevertheless,
Dreadnought, marked a change of era the
Royal Navy will never forget.

Dreadnought △   ▽ Onyx

Patrol Submarines

Type: Patrol Submarine					*Class:* "Oberon"

Name	No.	Builders	Laid down	Launched	Commissioned
OBERON	S 09	HM Dockyard, Chatham	28 Nov 1957	18 July 1959	24 Feb 1961
ODIN	S 10	Cammell Laird & Co Ltd, Birkenhead	27 April 1959	4 Nov 1960	3 May 1962
ORPHEUS	S 11	Vickers (Shipbuilding) Ltd, Barrow-in-Furness	16 April 1959	17 Nov 1959	25 Nov 1960
OLYMPUS	S 12	Vickers (Shipbuilding) Ltd, Barrow-in-Furness	4 Mar 1960	14 June 1961	7 July 1962
OSIRIS*	S 13	Vickers (Shipbuilding) Ltd, Barrow-in-Furness	26 Jan 1962	29 Nov 1962	11 Jan 1964
ONSLAUGHT	S 14	HM Dockyard, Chatham	8 April 1959	24 Sept 1960	14 Aug 1962
OTTER*	S 15	Scotts (Shipbuilding) Co Ltd, Greenock	14 Jan 1960	15 May 1961	20 Aug 1962
ORACLE*	S 16	Cammell Laird & Co Ltd, Birkenhead	26 April 1960	26 Sept 1961	14 Feb 1963
OCELOT*	S 17	HM Dockyard, Chatham	17 Nov 1960	5 May 1962	31 Jan 1964
OTUS*	S 18	Scotts (Shipbuilding) Co Ltd, Greenock	31 May 1961	17 Oct 1962	5 Oct 1963
OPOSSUM	S 19	Cammell Laird & Co Ltd, Birkenhead	21 Dec 1961	23 May 1963	5 June 1964
OPPORTUNE	S 20	Scotts (Shipbuilding) Co Ltd, Greenock	26 Oct 1962	14 Feb 1964	29 Dec 1964
ONYX	S 21	Cammell Laird & Co Ltd, Birkenhead	16 Nov 1964	18 Aug 1966	20 Nov 1967

*Refit

Displacement, tons: 1,610 standard; 2,030 surfaced; 2,410 dived
Length, feet (metres): 241 (73.5) pp; 295.2 (90.0) oa
Beam, feet (metres): 26.5 (8.1)

Draught, feet (metres): 18 (5.5)
Torpedo tubes: 8 × 21-in (533 mm) (6 bow, 2 stern); 24 torpedoes carried
Main machinery: 2 Admiralty Standard Range 1, 16 VMS diesels; 3,680 bhp;

2 electric motors; 6,000 shp; 2 shafts
Speed, knots: 12 surfaced; 17 dived
Complement: 68 (6 officers and 62 men)

This improvement on the "Porpoise" class

was chiefly notable for variations in the form of the deep-frames supporting the pressure hull and in the use of reinforced plastic for the casing and, in some cases, the fin. It was strange for some elderly submariners to see the sun shining through the conning tower for a change.

So successful was this design that overseas orders came from Australia, Brazil, Canada and Chile, a good buy as this was probably the best diesel-propelled submarine then designed. A somewhat peculiar situation arose when some of this class were operating in the Seventh Submarine Squadron in Singapore during the period known as Indonesian Confrontation in the mid-1960s. The possibility of meeting potentially hostile small craft whilst on the surface resulted in some of these boats being fitted with 20-mm guns for which they were not designed and ill-adapted. Their proper area of operations was in deep waters where full value could be obtained from their very efficient sonar sets.

Type: Patrol Submarine (SS)					*Class:* "Porpoise"
Name	*No.*	*Builders*	*Laid down*	*Launched*	*Commissioned*
PORPOISE	S 01	Vickers (Shipbuilding) Ltd, Barrow-in-Furness	15 June 1954	25 April 1956	17 April 1958
FINWHALE	S 05	Cammell Laird & Co Ltd, Birkenhead	18 Sept 1956	21 July 1959	19 Aug 1960
SEALION	S 07	Cammell Laird & Co Ltd, Birkenhead	5 June 1958	31 Dec 1959	25 July 1961
WALRUS	S 08	Scotts (Shipbuilding) Co Ltd, Greenock	12 Feb 1958	22 Sept 1959	10 Feb 1961

Displacement, tons: 1,610 standard; 2,030 surfaced; 2,410 dived
Length, feet (metres): 241 (73.5) pp; 295.2 (90.0) oa
Beam, feet (metres): 26.5 (8.1)
Draught, feet (metres): 18 (5.5)
Torpedo tubes: 8 × 21-in (533 mm) (6 bow, 2 stern); 30 torpedoes carried
Main machinery: 2 Admiralty Standard Range 1, 16 VMS diesels; 3,680 bhp; 2 electric motors; 6,000 shp; 2 shafts
Speed, knots: 12 surfaced; 17 dived
Complement: 71 (6 officers and 65 men)

The progression of future submarine design from the large numbers of "S, T, U" and "V" classes which bore the brunt of war patrols from 1939-45 was in a series of hiccups. The "A" class was built for service in the Pacific and given high surface speed to profit from American experience. Soon after the last of these was completed in 1948 the lessons learned from the German "Type XXI" class were applied to the "T-boats". Eight were cut in half, given an extra battery section and streamlined, thus giving them a dived speed of over 15 knots. Five other "T-boats", with rivetted as opposed to welded hulls, were streamlined (T-streamlines) with a reasonable increase

of dived speed. Barely were the last of the "T"-class conversions finished before the first of the pair of "E" class (*Explorer* and *Excalibur*) was completed in November 1956. She incorporated a High-Test-Peroxide plant driving steam turbines but her completion came nearly two years after the introduction of nuclear power in the USN. With a large number of A-boats available, the RN started a programme of streamlining this class in 1955, the result being almost indistinguishable from the T-conversions except for the bulge for the gun-tower hatch forward of the fin. These were all planned to mount their 4-inch gun if necessary, as were their predecessors of the T-streamline period. Several of the A-boats were thus-armed during Indonesian Confrontation in the mid-1960s.

But a totally new design had been gestating and this reached fruition with the completion of *Porpoise* in April 1958.

A-boats were still being streamlined but the eight boats of this new class were far ahead of their predecessors in hull design, electrical layout and diving depth. They were a new generation of diesel-submarines coming at a time when nuclear propulsion had provided a gigantic leap in the concept of submarine operations. But they were still excellent conventional submarines with a continuing part to play in the overall strategic picture.

Finwhale

Amphibious Warfare Forces

Type: Assault Ship					Class: "Fearless"

Name	No.	Builders	Laid down	Launched	Commissioned
FEARLESS	L 10 (ex-L 3004)	Harland & Wolff Ltd, Belfast	25 July 1962	19 Dec 1963	25 Nov 1965
INTREPID	L 11 (ex-L 3005)	John Brown & Co (Clydebank) Ltd	19 Dec 1962	25 June 1964	11 Mar 1967

Displacement, tons: 11,060 standard; 12,120 full load; 16,950 ballasted
Length, feet (metres): 500 (152.4) wl; 520 (158.5) oa
Beam, feet (metres): 80 (24.4)
Draught, feet (metres): 20.5 (6.2)
Draught, ballasted: 32 (9.8) aft; 23 (7.0) fwd
Landing craft: 4 LCM(9) in dock; 4 LCVP at davits
Vehicles: Specimen load: 15 tanks,

7 three-ton and 20 quarter-ton trucks
Aircraft: Flight deck facilities for 5 Wessex helicopters
Missiles: 4 Seacat systems
Guns: 2 × 40-mm Bofors
Main engines: 2 EE turbines; 22,000 shp; 2 shafts
Boilers: 2 Babcock & Wilcox
Speed, knots: 21
Range, miles: 5,000 at 20 knots
Complement: 580 (380-400 with 700 for

short hauls)

These ships were ordered and designed when it was still a political assumption that Great Britain would retain her responsibilities abroad and would be prepared to fulfil NATO obligations to operate on the Northern or Southern flank of that alliance. The provision of only two ships was inadequate to ensure one in full running order at any one time but when they finally

Intrepid ▽   △ Fearless

commissioned in 1965/67 they were a valuable addition to the amphibious capability of the RN.

The landing-ship had been developed in the USA from original British designs of World War II and the concept had been advanced in the fifteen Dock Landing Ships (LSD) of the "Casa Grande" class which were commissioned at Newport News and Boston in 1944-45. These had a docking well 392 feet long and were designed to carry 3 LCUs or 18 LSMs or 32 LVTs (amphibious tractors) as well as having a helicopter platform. This class was appreciably smaller than the "Fearless" class with a full load tonnage of 9,375 compared with 12,120, although the four succeeding US designs which were completed between 1954 and 1972 eventually raised this to 17,300 tons. The advantages of large-scale production can be seen in the capital costs of ships of the two countries – *Fearless* £11,250,000 with the larger and later US "Anchorage" class costing less than £5,000,000.

Each ship is fitted out with an Assault Operations Room for combined control of any such task and with a flight deck capability for five helicopters. They could operate effectively alone in a minor intervention role. At present one is maintained in reserve while the second is used for sea-training of officers from the Britannia Royal Naval College, Dartmouth.

Type: Logistic Landing Ship   *Class:* "Sir Lancelot"

Name	No.	Builders	Laid down	Launched	Commissioned
SIR BEDIVERE	L 3004	Hawthorn Leslie	Oct 1965	20 July 1966	18 May 1967
SIR GALAHAD	L 3005	Alex Stephen	Feb 1965	19 April 1966	17 Dec 1966
SIR GERAINT	L 3027	Alex Stephen	June 1965	26 Jan 1967	12 July 1967
SIR LANCELOT	L 3029	Fairfield	Mar 1962	25 June 1963	16 Jan 1964
SIR PERCIVAL	L 3036	Hawthorn Leslie	April 1966	4 Oct 1967	23 Mar 1968
SIR TRISTRAM	L 3505	Hawthorn Leslie	Feb 1966	12 Dec 1966	14 Sept 1967

Displacement, tons: 3,270 light; 5,674 full load; (3,370 and 5,550 in *Sir Lancelot*)

Dimensions, feet (metres): 366.3 (120) pp; 412.1 oa × 59.8 × 13.0 (135.1 × 19.6 × 4.3)

Guns: Fitted for 2 × 40-mm – not normally carried

Sir Percival △   ▽ Sir Geraint

Main engines: 2 Mirrlees Diesels;
9,400 bhp; 2 shafts;
(2 Denny/Sulzer diesels;
9,520 bhp in *Sir Lancelot*)
Speed, knots: 17
Oil fuel, tons: 815
Range, miles: 8,000 at 15 knots
Complement: 68 (18 officers and 50 ratings)
Military lift: 340

These impressive looking ships were originally built for the Army, *Sir Lancelot* being the prototype and varying in detail from the rest of the class. Facilities are available for bow or stern loading with ramps provided for access from deck to deck. Helicopters can be operated from both the well-deck and after platform under all conditions in all but *Sir Lancelot* where the well-deck is suitable only for fair-weather

day conditions. If required to carry helicopters for transfer eleven can be stowed on the Tank Deck and nine on the Vehicle Deck.

All vehicles can be maintained on board and the ships are capable of laying out pontoon equipment.

Transferred to the RFA in early 1970.

Type: Logistic Landing Craft (RCT) *Class:* "Ardennes"

Name	No.	Builders	Laid down	Launched	Commissioned
ARDENNES	L 4001	Brooke Marine, Lowestoft	27 Aug 1975	29 July 1976	1977
ARAKAN	L —	Brooke Marine, Lowestoft	16 Feb 1976	23 May 1977	1978

Displacement, tons: 870 standard;
1,413 full load
Dimensions, feet (metres):
237.5 oa × 46 × 5.8 (72.4 × 14 × 1.8)
Main engines: 2 diesels;
2,000 bhp = 10.3 knots

Range, miles: 4Z000 at 10 knots
Complement: 35 (plus 34 troops)

These two rather startling looking ships were ordered for the RCT in October 1974. Their low speed makes them suitable only for

individual running between Army points of embarkation/landing, and can carry 350 tonnes of stores or 5 Chieftain tanks.

Type: Landing Craft (LCT) *Class:* "LCT (8)"

Name		
AGHEILA L 4002		
ABBEVILLE L 4041		
AUDEMER L 4061		

Displacement, tons: 657 light; 895 to 1,017 loaded

Dimensions, feet (metres):
231.2 oa × 39 × 3.2 forward; 5 aft

(70.5 × 11.9 × 1 forward; 1.8 aft) Beaching draughts

Main engines: 4 Paxman diesels; 1,840 bhp = 12.6 knots
Complement: 33 to 37

Originally there were nine of these classic type of war-time LCTs which were transferred from the RN to the RCT but old-age has reduced the numbers to three. Now being replaced by the "Ardennes" class.

Abbeville △   ▽ Agheila

Type: (LST)   *Class:* "LST(3)"

Name
EMPIRE GULL (ex-*Trouncer*) L 3513

Displacement, tons: 2,260 light; 4,960 full load
Measurement, tons: 4,257.9 gross
Dimensions, feet (metres): 347 × 54.1 × 12 (105.8 × 16.5 × 3.7)
Main engines: 2 Triple Expansion; 2 shafts;

5,500 shp = 10 knots
Boilers: 2 Water Tube
Oil fuel, tons: 950
Complement: 63 officers and men
Troop accommodation: 8 officers, 72 ORs

This last survivor of one of the most numerous of landing ships of World War II has been threatened with deletion for some years but was due to pay-off in 1978. RFA manned, with a Chinese crew. Built in Quebec in 1945.

Empire Gull

Type: Landing Craft   *Class:* "LCM(9)"

Name	No.	Builders	Commissioned
—	L 700	Brooke Marine Ltd	1964
—	L 701	Brooke Marine Ltd	1964
—	L 702	Brooke Marine Ltd	1965
—	L 703	Brooke Marine Ltd	1965
—	L 704	R. Dunston (Thorne)	1964
—	L 705	R. Dunston (Thorne)	1965
—	L 706	R. Dunston (Thorne)	1965
—	L 707	R. Dunston (Thorne)	1965
—	L 708	R. Dunston (Thorne)	1966
—	L 709	R. Dunston (Thorne)	1966
—	L 710	J. Bolson (Poole)	1965
—	L 711	J. Bolson (Poole)	1965
—	L 3507	Vosper Ltd	1963
—	L 3508	Vosper Ltd	1963

Displacement, tons: 75 light; 176 loaded
Dimensions, feet (metres):
85 oa × 21.5 × 5.5 (25.7 × 6.5 × 1.7)
Capacity: 2 tanks or 100 tons of vehicles
Main engines: 2 Paxman 6-cylinder YHXAM diesels; 2 shafts; 624 bhp = 10 knots. Screws enclosed in Kort nozzles to improve manoeuvrability

"LCM(9)" 3507 and 3508 were the first minor landing-craft built in the UK after World War II. They have the traditional ramped bow and an enclosed wheel-house fitted with radar. The first two were used for evaluation trials and are now run by the RCT. Of the remainder four each are allocated to *Fearless* and *Intrepid*.

L709

3507

Type: Landing Craft
Class: "LCM(7)"

Name
7037
7100

Displacement, tons: 28 light; 63 loaded
Dimensions, feet (metres): 60.2 × 16 × 3.7
(18.4 × 4.9 × 1.2)

Main engines: 290 bhp = 9.8 knots

Now employed as naval servicing craft and

store carriers. They have been re-engined
with Gray diesels.

Type: Landing Craft (LCVP)
Class: "LCVP(1) (2) and (3)"

Name
LCVP (1) 102, 112, 118, 120, 123, 127, 128, 134, 136
LCVP (2) 142-149
LCVP (3) 150-158

Displacement, tons: 8.5 light; 13.5 full load
Dimensions, feet (metres):
41.5 (LCVP (2)); 43 (LCVP (3)) × 10 × 2.5
(12.7; 13.1 × 3.1 × 0.8)
Main engines: 130 bhp = 8 knots;

2 Foden diesels; 200 bhp = 10 knots
(LCVP (2))

LCVP(2)s carried by *Fearless* and *Intrepid*
can carry 35 troops or 2 Land-Rovers with a

crew of 4. In 1966 LCA(2)s were
redesignated LCVPs (Landing Craft Vehicle
and Personnel).

Type: Landing Craft (RCT)   *Class:* "River"

Name
AVON RPL 01
BUDE RPL 02
CLYDE RPL 03
DART RPL 04
EDEN RPL 05
FORTH RPL 06
GLEN RPL 07
HAMBLE RPL 08
KENNET RPL 10
LODDON RPL 11
MEDWAY RPL 12

These eleven LCMs are run by the RCT as store support carriers.

Type: Landing Craft   *Class:* "LCP(L)3"

Name
LCP (L) (3) 501, 503, 556

Displacement, tons: 6.5 light; 10 loaded
Dimensions, feet (metres): 37 × 11 × 3.2

(11.3 × 3.4 × 1)
Main engines: 225 bhp = 12 knots

Used as general utility craft.

Helicopter Support Ship

Type: Helicopter Support Ship   *Class:* ??

Name	No.	Builders	Commissioned
ENGADINE	K 08	Henry Robb Ltd, Leith	15 Dec 1967

Displacement, tons: 8,000 full load
Measurement, tons: 6,384 gross; 2,848 net
Dimensions, feet (metres):
424.0 oa × 58.4 × 22.1 (129.3 × 17.8 × 6.7)
Aircraft: 4 Wessex and 2 Wasp or Sea King
helicopters
Main engines: 1 Sulzer two-stroke,
5-cylinder turbocharged 5RD68 diesel;
5,500 bhp = 14.5 knots
Complement: RFA: 71 (18 officers and 53
men); RN: 26 (4 officers and 22 ratings)
Accommodation for a further RN 109
(25 officers and 84 ratings)

At a time when the increased speed of
submarines required exercises to be
conducted in deep water well beyond the
range of helicopters from Portland there was
a need for a ship to carry these aircraft to
their operating area. Manpower restraints
would not allow a large enough ship's
company for an RN ship of the requisite
size. With experience of aircraft operating
from both merchant ships and RFAs it was
suggested that a combination of RFA/RN
manning could ease the burden but this
solution was by no means popular. However

necessity won the day and *Engadine* was
ordered in August 1964. Despite rather less
speed than originally hoped for she has
done a magnificent job since commissioning
in December 1967. In 1969 she was fitted
with an additional small hangar for twelve
pilotless target aircraft and in 1977 made
her own impressive appearance second
behind the Royal Yacht at Her Majesty's
Jubilee Review in the Solent.

Engadine

Type: Mine Warfare Support Ship

Class: "Abdiel"

Name	No.	Builders	Commissioned
ABDIEL	N 21	John I. Thorneycroft Ltd, Woolston, Southampton	17 Oct 1967

Displacement, tons: 1,375 standard; 1,500 full load
Dimensions, feet (metres): 244.5 pp; 265 oa × 38.5 × 10 (80.2; 86.8 × 12.6 × 3.3)
Mines: 44 carried
Main engines: 2 Paxman Ventura 16-cylinder pressure charged diesels;

1,250 rpm; 2,690 bhp = 16 knots
Complement: 77

As the much-loved *Plover* reached the end of her long life it was apparent that a new ship would have to relieve her, if only as an exercise minelayer. So in June 1965 *Abdiel*

was ordered, a multi-role ship designed not only for the minelaying task but also as an MCM support ship with spare sweeps on reels and a crane to cope with engineering problems. She has well merited the £1,500,000 spent on her construction.

Abdiel

Type: Minehunter

Class: "Hunt"

Name	No.	Builders	Commissioned
BRECON	M 29	Vosper Thornycroft Ltd	1978
LEDBURY	—	Vosper Thornycroft Ltd	—

Displacement, tons: 615 standard; 725 full load
Dimensions, feet (metres): 197 × 32.3 × 7.3 (60 × 9.9 × 2.2)
Main engines: 2 Ruston-Paxman Deltic diesels; 3,540 bhp = 17 knots
Complement: 45

With *Wilton* as a prototype this class of mine countermeasures vessels were ordered with *Brecon* being laid down on

15 September 1975. This was thirteen years to the month since the idea of using Glass Reinforced Plastic (GRP) for the hull of the new generation of minesweepers had first been raised – the only difference was that inflation of both money and technology had raised the price from some £3 million to £8 million with a possible doubling now of the latter figure. The result may well be an inadequate number of such ships to ensure the clearance of even our major ports. Past

experience has shown that, if mine clearance forces are needed, they are needed in droves and minewarfare is a subtle, clandestine operation which can be carried out with no declaration of war. Minesweeping or hunting is a wearying occupation both physically and mentally – new methods are needed if Britain's ports can be provided with a surety of operation. These ships are being provided with two French PAP 104 mine destructor outfits.

Type: Minesweeper/Minehunter (Coastal)   *Class:* "Wilton"

Name	No.	Builders	Commissioned
WILTON	M 1116	Vosper Thornycroft, Woolston	14 July 1973

Displacement, tons: 450 standard
Dimensions, feet (metres):
153.0 oa × 28.8 × 8.5 (46.3 × 8.8 × 2.5)
Gun: 1 × 40-mm Mark VII
Main engines: 2 English Electric Deltic 18 diesels; 2 shafts; 3,000 bhp = 16 knots
Complement: 37 (5 officers and 32 ratings)

Wilton was the first warship in non-Communist navies with a hull built of Glass Reinforced Plastic (GRP). She was built at the same time as the first of the Soviet "Zhenya" class, another prototype MCM vessel. The contract for her construction was signed with Vosper

Thornycroft on 11 February 1970 and she was subsequently fitted with the reconditioned main engines and equipment of the scrapped "Ton" class minesweeper HMS *Derriton*. After trials she was employed in the mine-clearance operations in the Suez Canal in the autumn of 1974.

Wilton

Type: Minehunter/Minesweeper – Coastal   *Class:* "Ton"

Name	No.	Builders	Commissioned
Minehunters			
BILDESTON*	M 1110	J. S. Doig (Grimsby) Ltd)	28 April 1953
BRERETON	M 1113	Richards Ironworks	9 July 1954
BRINTON	M 1114	Cook Welton and Gemmell	4 Mar 1954
BRONINGTON	M 1115	Cook Welton and Gemmell	4 June 1954
BOSSINGTON	M 1133	J. I. Thornycroft & Co, Southampton	11 Dec 1956
GAVINGTON	M 1140	J. S. Doig (Grimsby) Ltd	14 July 1954
HUBBERSTON	M 1147	Fleetlands Shipyards Ltd, London	14 Oct 1955
IVESTON	M 1151	Philip & Sons Ltd, Dartmouth	29 June 1955
KEDLESTON†	M 1153	William Pickersgill & Son	2 July 1955
KELLINGTON†	M 1154	William Pickersgill & Son	4 Nov 1955
KIRKLISTON	M 1157	Harland & Wolff Ltd, Belfast	21 Aug 1954
MAXTON	M 1165	Harland & Wolff Ltd, Belfast	19 Feb 1957
NURTON	M 1166	Harland & Wolff Ltd, Belfast	21 Aug 1957
SHERATON	M 1181	White's Shipyard Ltd, Southampton	24 Aug 1956
SHOULTON	M 1182	Montrose Shipyard Ltd	16 Nov 1965
*Refit †RNR			

Name	No.	Builders	Commissioned
Minesweepers (coastal)			
ALFRISTON	M 1103	J. I. Thornycroft & Co, Southampton	16 Mar 1954
BICKINGTON	M 1109	White's Shipyard Ltd, Southampton	27 May 1954
CRICHTON	M 1124	J. S. Doig (Grimsby) Ltd	23 April 1954
CUXTON	M 1125	Camper and Nicholson Ltd, Gosport	1953
GLASSERTON	M 1141	J. S. Doig (Grimsby) Ltd)	31 Dec 1954
HODGESTON†	M 1146	Fleetlands Shipyards Ltd, London	17 Dec 1954
LALESTON	M 1158	Harland & Wolff	1954
REPTON†	M 1167	Harland & Wolff Ltd, Belfast	12 Dec 1957
POLLINGTON	M 1173	Camper & Nicholson Ltd, Gosport	5 Sept 1958
SHAVINGTON	M 1180	White's Shipyard Ltd, Southampton	1 Mar 1956
UPTON†	M 1187	J. I. Thornycroft & Co, Southampton	24 July 1956
WALKERTON	M 1188	J. I. Thornycroft & Co, Southampton	10 Jan 1958
WOTTON*	M 1195	Philip & Sons Ltd, Dartmouth	13 June 1957
SOBERTON	M 1200	Fleetlands Shipyards Ltd, Gosport	17 Sept 1957
STUBBINGTON	M 1204	Camper & Nicholson Ltd, Gosport	30 July 1957
WISTON	M 1205	Wivenhoe Shipyard Ltd	17 Feb 1960
LEWISTON	M 1208	Herd & Mackenzie, Buckie, Banff	16 June 1960
CROFTON†	M 1216	J. I. Thornycroft & Co, Southampton	26 Aug 1958
*Refit †RNS			

Displacement, tons: 360 standard; 425 full load
Dimensions, feet (metres): 140.0 pp; 153.0 oa × 28.8 × 8.2 (42.7; 46.3 × 8.8 × 2.5)
Guns: Vary in different ships, some sweepers having no 40-mm, some 1 × 40-mm whilst hunters have 1 or 2 × 40-mm; 2 × 20-mm
Main engines: 2 diesels; 2 shafts; 2,500 bhp (JVSS 12 Mirrlees), 3,000 bhp (18A-7A Deltic)
Speed, knots: 15
Oil fuel, tons: 45
Range, miles: 2,300 at 13 knots
Complement: 29 (38 in minehunters, 5 officers and 33 ratings)

Alarm was generated in the Admiralty when knowledge of a new type of Soviet mine was gained during the Korean War of 1950-53. As a result an unparalleled peacetime building programme of 118 "Ton" class minesweepers and 105 inshore minesweepers was put in hand. John I. Thornycroft & Co. Ltd. was the lead yard for the coastal minesweepers built with double-hulls of mahogany. These hulls were originally sheathed with copper which, in many cases, was replaced by Cascover nylon sheathing to prolong their hull-lives. A further alteration took place when, in the early 1960s, the advent of the Type 193 minehunting sonar brought the conversion of fifteen of this class for minehunting duties. This involved the replacement, where required, of the Mirrlees diesels by Deltics and the fitting of diving facilities as well as the new sonar.

Ships of this class have been transferred to Argentina (6), Australia (6), Ghana (1), India (4), Ireland (3), Malaysia (7) and South Africa (10).

Until recently, eleven of this class were deployed amongst the RNR units of the UK, having their names changed temporarily to those of their parent units. This practice has now been dropped and six of these CMS work with the RNR in area groupings retaining their own names. Ten others are employed on fishery protection duties whilst a further five, which were converted for patrol duties in 1971, form the 6th Patrol Squadron at Hong Kong.

Iveston △

▽ Lewiston

Type: Minesweeper (Inshore) **Class:** "Ham" (M2601 and 2793 series)

Name	No.	Builders	Commissioned
DITTISHAM	M 2621	Fairlie Yacht Slip	1954
FLINTHAM	M 2628	Bolson & Co	1955
THORNHAM (Aberdeen)	M 2793	Taylor, Shoreham	1957

Displacement, tons: 120 standard;
159 full load
Dimensions, feet (metres): 2601 Series:
100 pp; 106.5 oa × 21.2 × 5.5 (30.5;
32.4 × 6.5 × 1.7); 2793 Series: 100 pp;
107.5 oa × 22 × 5.8 (30.5; 32.1 × 6.6 × 1.8)
Gun: 1 × 20-mm Oerlikon forward
Main engines: 2 Paxman diesels;
1,100 bhp = 14 knots
Oil fuel, tons: 15
Complement: 15 (2 officers and 13 ratings)

At the same time as the "Ton" class coastal minesweepers were designed two classes of Inshore Minesweepers were also put in hand. Ninety-five of the "Ham" class were eventually built, the first, *Inglesham*, being launched by J. Samuel White & Co. Ltd, Cowes in April 1952. The vessels of the 2601 series were of composite construction, those of the 2793 series of wood.

When their future came under review in the early 1960s it was decided to convert a number for duties other than minesweeping, thus saving new construction costs. Two (*Waterwitch, ex-Powderham* and *Woodlark, ex-Yaxham*) were converted for inshore surveying, six for Torpedo Recovery duties, six for service with the RN Auxiliary Service (RNXS) and three as de-gaussing vessels.

Foreign transfers between 1955 and 1968 included Australia (3), France (15), Ghana (2), India (2), Libya (2), Malaysia (4), South Yemen (3).

Thornham is attached to Aberdeen University RNU.

Flintham △   ▽ Isis

Type: Minehunter (Inshore)   *Class:* "Ley" (M2001 Series)

Name	No.	Builders	Commissioned
AVELEY	M 2002	J. S. White & Co Ltd, Cowes	1953
ISIS (ex-*Cradley*)	M 2010	Saunders Roe Ltd	1955

Displacement, tons: 123 standard; 164 full load
Dimensions, feet (metres): 100 pp; 107 oa × 21.8 × 5.5 (30.5; 32.3 × 6.5 × 1.7)
Gun: 1 × 40-mm or 1 × 20-mm (forward)
Main engines: 2 Paxman diesels; 700 bhp = 13 knots

Complement: 15 (2 officers and 13 ratings)

These two minesweepers are the survivors of a class of ten built at the same time as the "Ham" class. Their construction was composite (wood and metal) with superstructures differing in silhouette and had no winch or sweeping gear, being built as minehunters. *Aveley* is attached to HM Naval Base, Plymouth and *Isis* (renamed in 1963) has been attached to Southampton University RNU since April 1974 after a period of RNR service.

Maintenance Ships

Type: Maintenance Ship   Class: Ex-"Colossus"

Name	No.	Builders	Laid down	Launched	Commissioned
TRIUMPH	A 108 (ex-R 16)	R & W Hawthorn Leslie, Hebburn	27 Jan 1943	2 Oct 1944	9 April 1946

Displacement, tons: 13,500 standard; 17,500 full load
Length, feet (metres): 630.0 (192.0) pp; 650.0 (198.1) wl; 699.0 (231.1) oa
Beam, feet (metres): 80.0 (24.4)
Draught, feet (metres): 23.7 (7.2)
Width, feet (metres): 112.5 (34.3) oa
Aircraft: 3 helicopters in flight deck hangar
Guns: 4 × 40-mm; 3 saluting (now removed)
Main engines: Parsons geared turbines; 2 shafts; 40,000 shp
Boilers: 4 Admiralty 3-drum type; pressure 400 psi (28.1 kg/cm²); temperature 700°F (371°C)
Speed, knots: 24.25
Oil fuel, tons: 3,000
Range, miles: 10,000 at 14 knots; 5,500 at full speed
Complement: 500 (27 officers and 473 men) plus 285 (15 officers and 270 men) on maintenance staff

Originally completed as one of the ten "Colossus" class aircraft-carriers designed during World War II Triumph carried a complement of thirty-five aircraft and in the post-war years flew strikes with Seafires and Fireflies against the Communist insurgents in Malaya in 1949. In June 1950 she was the first British carrier involved in the Korean War, being relieved by Theseus in late-September. Another "first" was achieved in February 1952 when she had an angled-flight-deck layout painted on her existing deck and carried out the first landings with this new concept. At the time of Suez (1956) she was in reserve prior to conversion for training duties and in 1958 was once again taken in hand for further conversion, this time as a repair-ship.

Although the work involved took only 2½ years of dockyard time she was in hand from January 1958 until January 1965, her change being halted from time to time as other commitments came up. The Navy eventually received a ship capable of accommodating four Fleet Maintenance units, servicing and maintaining four frigates at one time, and providing helicopter servicing. At a conversion cost of £10,200,000 this is the very least that could have been expected.

She was employed in her support role during the latter part of Indonesian Confrontation, being based at Singapore, and subsequently moving to Mombasa to support the Beira patrol. With the Royal Navy's withdrawal from foreign waters she returned to Chatham where she is now in reserve.

Triumph

Type: Maintenance Ship   Class: "Head"

Name	No.	Builders	Laid down	Launched	Commissioned
RAME HEAD	A 134	Burrard DD Co, Vancouver	12 July 1944	22 Nov 1944	18 Aug 1945
BERRY HEAD	A 191	North Vancouver Ship Repairers	15 June 1944	21 Oct 1944	30 May 1945

Displacement, tons: 9,000 standard; 11,270 full load
Length, feet (metres): 416.0 (126.8) pp; 441.5 (134.6) oa
Beam, feet (metres): 57.5 (17.5)
Draught, feet (metres): 22.5 (6.9)
Guns: 11 × 40-mm
Main engines: Triple expansion; 2,500 ihp
Boilers: 2 Foster Wheeler

Speed, knots: 10 approx
Oil fuel, tons: 1,600 capacity
Complement: 425

During the later years of the war eleven maintenance ships of mercantile design were built in Canada; of these five were of the "Head" class. Beachy Head and Flamborough Head were transferred to the

RCN soon after World War II and of the three RN ships Berry Head and Rame Head were modernised in the 1960s. Duncansby Head was not so treated and was subsequently deleted. Rame Head became accommodation ship at Portsmouth in June 1976 and Berry Head is stationed at Plymouth.

Rame Head

Royal Yacht

Type: Royal Yacht   *Class:* "Britannia"

Name	No.	Builders	Laid down	Launched	Commissioned
BRITANNIA	A 00	John Brown & Co Ltd, Clydebank	July 1962	16 April 1953	14 Jan 1954

Displacement, tons: 3,990 light; 4,961 full load

Measurement, tons: 5,769 gross

Dimensions, feet (metres): 360.0 pp; 380.0 wl; 412.2 oa × 55.0 × 17.0 (109.8; 115.9; 125.7 × 16.8 × 5.2)

Main engines: Single reduction geared turbines; 2 shafts; 12,000 shp = 21 knots

Boilers: 2

Oil fuel, tons: 330 (490 with auxiliary fuel tanks)

Range, miles: 2,100 at 20 knots; 2,400 at 18 knots; 3,000 at 15 knots

Complement: 270

HMY *Britannia* was designed for the dual role of Royal Yacht and hospital ship. In the former guise she has probably logged more miles than most ships of her age and become a familiar sight throughout the world. Her immaculate appearance has been a continuing advertisement for a navy too rarely seen abroad these days.

There are certain peculiarities in her manning. She is the only RN ship commanded by a Rear-Admiral (Flag Officer Royal Yachts) and her company, the Yachtsmen, are drawn from a list of volunteers. Fitted with stabilisers she has undergone a number of refits and modifications one of which, in November 1958, included the hingeing of the upper sections of her fore and main masts to permit passage under the bridges of the St. Lawrence Seaway when it was opened by HM Queen Elizabeth II.

Britannia

Submarine Depot Ship

Type: Submarine Depot Ship					Class: "Maidstone"

Name	No.	Builders	Laid down	Launched	Commissioned
FORTH	A 187	John Brown, Clydebank	30 June 1937	11 Aug 1938	14 May 1939

Displacement, tons: 10,000 standard; 13,000 full load
Length, feet (metres): 497.0 (151.5) pp; 531.0 (161.8) oa
Beam, feet (metres): 73.0 (22.3)
Draught, feet (metres): 21.2 (6.5)
Guns: 5 × 40-mm Bofors
Main engines: Geared turbines (Brown Curtis)
Boilers: 4 Admiralty 3-drum type
Speed, knots: 16
Oil fuel, tons: 2,300
Complement: 695 (45 officers and 650 men) Accommodation for 1,159 (119 officers and 1,040 men)

At a time when the Royal Navy's submarines have been withdrawn to an inner perimeter it is worth recalling the depot ships which supported the Submarine Service throughout the preceding years. At the end of World War I the light-cruisers *Fearless* and *Ithuriel* were attached to the 1st and 2nd Flotillas while *Ambrose, Titania, Lucia, Pandora, Maidstone, Adamant, Alecto, Royal Arthur, St. George, Vulcan, Thames* and *Forth* acted as depot ships. They were soon to be joined by the repair ship *Cyclops* but between the wars their numbers were whittled down so that, by 1939, only *Titania, Lucia, Cyclops* and *Alecto* with her bowsprit remained. Of this company *Medway* of 14,650 tons was completed in September 1929 and, on the outbreak of war, was supporting thirteen submarines of the 4th Flotilla in China. Transferred to the Mediterranean she was sunk whilst on passage from Alexandria to Beirut in June 1942. Of an improved design *Maidstone* and *Forth* were completed in 1938 and 1939 respectively whilst *Adamant*, laid down in November 1940, was completed in February 1942.

In September 1939 the Home Fleet numbered *Forth* with the 2nd Flotilla of 10 boats at Dundee, *Titania* with the 6th Flotilla of 6 boats at Blyth and *Cyclops* with 9 S-boats of the 3rd Flotilla. *Alecto* supported the 5th Flotilla of 8 boats while *Cyclops* was engaged in other training work. In the Mediterranean *Maidstone* was depot ship for the ten boats of the 1st Flotilla. Thus six flotillas were deployed with their depot ships, an arrangement changed in February 1941 when *Forth* took up station at Halifax, Nova Scotia with four T-boats and, later, the mighty French *Surcouf*. This transfer was designed to provide submarine escorts for Atlantic convoys but, when this ill-conceived plan was seen to be a failure, *Forth* returned to the Holy Loch in Scotland.

The converted merchant-ship *Montclare* transferred to the Far East Fleet at Trincomalee and remained in service until 1958, sharing the main burden with *Adamant, Maidstone* and *Forth*. Later these ships split the submarine responsibilities with *Tyne* who for a time took over the Home Fleet submarines.

When the design of a new submarine depot ship was cancelled in the early 1960s *Maidstone* and *Forth* were converted to support nuclear submarines and *Adamant* was paid off. The first of these, after a period as depot ship in Belfast, was scrapped in 1977 while *Forth*, having completed her conversion in 1966 and then served in Singapore and Mombasa, returned to Plymouth where she served as the depot ship of the 2nd Submarine Squadron and the base ship for the maintenance facility of *Defiance*. Due for paying-off in 1978

Ice Patrol Ship

Type: Ice Patrol Ship

Name	No.	Builders	Laid down	Launched	Commissioned
ENDURANCE (ex-*Anita Dan*)	A 171	Krögerwerft, Rendsburg	1955	May 1956	Dec 1956

Displacement, tons: 3,600
Measurement, tons: 2,641 gross
Length, feet (metres): 273.5 (89.7) pp; 300 (91.44) oa; 305 (92.96); including helicopter deck extension
Beam, feet (metres): 46 (14.02)
Draught, feet (metres): 18 (5.5)
Aircraft: 2 Whirlwind Mk IX helicopters
Guns: 2 × 20-mm
Main engines: 1 Babcock & Wilcox 550 VTBF diesel; 3,220 hp; 1 shaft
Speed, knots: 14.5
Range, miles: 12,000 at 14.5 knots

Complement: 119 (13 officers and 106 men, including a small Royal Marine detachment) plus 12 spare berths for scientists

In 1945 the Second British Grahamland Expedition was the fore-runner of a series of scientific expeditions under the aegis of the Foreign Office. As an additional support for the various research ships in the area *Guardian* (an ex-netlayer) was deployed to the Antarctic in the southern summer months. As her hull life was expiring in the early 1960s, plans were proposed for an icebreaker to relieve her but, as there were no British designs for such a ship and Finnish designs were not acceptable, these plans came to nothing. In 1967 *Anita Dan*, built in Germany in 1955-56, was bought from J Lauritzen Lines, Copenhagen and, converted by Harland and Wolff in 1967-68 for naval use, she has operated ever since as the support ship *Endurance* for the British Antarctic Survey, as a surveying ship in her own right and as a British presence in the Falklands area. She is notable for her red hull, a recognition device in iced-up areas.

Endurance

Hovercraft

Type: Hovercraft   *Class:* "Winchester" (SR.N6)

Displacement, tons: 10 normal gross weight

Dimensions, feet (metres):
48.4 × 23.0 × 15.0 oa (height); 4.0 (skirt)
(14.8 × 7 × 4.6; 1.3)

Main engines: 1 Rolls Royce Gnome gas-turbine; 900 shp = 50 knots

Range, miles: 200

The original Cockerell design of the Hovercraft was received with caution by the Board of Admiralty. Despite frequent suggestions as to its value for patrol, amphibious and mine-countermeasures duties it is now twenty years since the inception of the hovercraft and the Royal Navy is continuing "trials and evaluation." Over the last ten years the US Navy has spent over $300,000,000 on development of the "Surface Effect Ship" (SES). At the same time the USSR has been carrying out a series of trials which have resulted in the building of three 15-ton research hovercraft, some 30 "Gus" class with a carrying capacity of 50 marines, five of the 220-ton "Aist" class of about the same size as the British civilian SR. N4, used for cross-Channel services and the huge Ekranoplan W1G.

Type: Hovercraft   *Class:* "Wellington" (BHN.N7)

Displacement, tons: 50 max weight; 33 light

Dimensions, feet (metres):
78.3 × 45.5 × 34.0 oa (height); 5.5 (skirt)
(23.9 × 13 × 10.4; 1.7)

Main engines: 1 Rolls Royce Proteus gas-turbine; 4,250 shp = 60 knots

Complement: 14 plus trials crew

This machine was delivered to the Inter-Service Hovercraft Trials Unit in April 1970. Despite a number of records established in the intervening seven years little reaction has been noticeable in the Defence Estimates.

Type: Hovercraft   *Class:* SR. N 5

A small hovercraft used for crew training.

Diving Trials Ship

Type: Diving Ship   *Class:* "King Salvor"

Name	No.	Builders	Commissioned
RECLAIM (ex-*Salverdant*)	A 231	Wm Simons & Co Ltd, Renfrew	Oct 1948

Displacement, tons: 1,200 standard; 1,800 full load
Dimensions, feet (metres): 220 pp; 217.8 oa × 38 × 15.5 (61; 66.4 × 11.6 × 4.7)
Main engines: Triple expansion; 2 shafts; 1,500 ihp = 12 knots
Oil fuel, tons: 310
Range, miles: 3,000
Complement: 100

Despite nearly thirty years of service *Reclaim* was one of the best turned-out ships at the Jubilee Review of 1977, a reflection of the enthusiasm of those who run her and are trained in her. Her design was based on the "King Salvor" class of naval ocean salvage vessels and she was the first deep-diving and submarine rescue vessel designed as such for the Royal Navy. Her service includes an impressive list of diving records but she is now a reluctantly ageing old lady whose speed is insufficient for submarine rescue. She is due for replacement although no successor has yet been named. A design contract, however, has been placed with Scotts of Greenock.

Reclaim △▽

Light Forces

Type: Offshore Patrol Craft   **Class:** "Island"

Name	No.	Builders	Commissioned
JERSEY	P 295	Hall Russell & Co Ltd	15 Oct 1976
GUERNSEY	P 297	Hall Russell & Co Ltd	28 Oct 1977
SHETLAND	P 298	Hall Russell & Co Ltd	14 July 1977
ORKNEY	P 299	Hall Russell & Co Ltd	25 Feb 1977
LINDISFARNE	P 300	Hall Russell & Co Ltd	1978

Displacement, tons: 925 standard; 1,250 full load
Dimensions, feet (metres):
195.3 oa × 35.8 × 14 (59.6 × 10.9 × 4.3)
Gun: 1 × 40-mm
Main engines: 2 diesels; 1 shaft;
4,380 hp = 16 knots
Range, miles: 7,000 at 12 knots
Complement: 34

When the Government realised the need for some form of protection for the oil and gas-rigs which would be a salvation for the British balance-of-payments in the next fifteen years they had no ships suitable for the task. The re-commissioning of an antique tug *Reward* and the loan of a fishery protection ship, *Jura,* by the Scottish Department of Agriculture and Fisheries went some way to plugging the gap. By early 1976 sufficient unspent funds were available from the previous year's estimates to allow the ordering of five craft of similar design to *Jura*. This design was by no means ideal for patrolling a 200-mile Exclusive Economic Zone (EEZ) but was reasonably adequate for fishery protection, the original intention of the designers. Two more of this class were ordered later. The builders have since produced plans for a much-improved version of the "Islands" – it must be a matter of time to see how this idea is accepted by the Government.

Type: Large Patrol Craft   **Class:** "Bird"

Name	No.	Builders	Commissioned
KINGFISHER	P 260	R. Dunston Ltd, Hessle	8 Oct 1975
CYGNET	P 261	R. Dunston Ltd, Hessle	8 July 1976
PETEREL†	P 262	R. Dunston Ltd, Hessle	7 Feb 1977
SANDPIPER†	P 263	R. Dunston Ltd, Hessle	16 Sept 1977
†RNR			

Displacement, tons: 190
Dimensions, feet (metres):
120 oa × 23.0 × 6.5 (36.6 × 7.0 × 2)
Guns: 1 × 40-mm; 2 MG
Main engines: 2 Paxman 16 YJCM diesels;
4,200 bhp = 21 knots
Oil fuel, tons: 35
Range, miles: 2,000 at 14 knots
Complement: 24

The design of these craft is based on the smaller "Seal" class built for the RAF by Brooke Marine. Additions have been made to improve their sea-keeping qualities but their behaviour in a heavy sea-way remains as suspect as their cost, which the Government steadfastly refused to reveal until it was acknowledged that they had cost over £7,000,000 each. Reports of the former vary from "vile" to "unsatisfactory" so it is little surprise that they are considered unsuitable for all-the-year-round fishery protection duties. *Peterel* and *Sandpiper* are employed on RNR training and the other pair are attached to the 1st MCM Squadron at Rosyth.

Kingfisher

Type: Fast Training Boat

Class: "Scimitar"

Name	No.	Builders	Commissioned
SCIMITAR	P 271	Vosper Thornycroft Group, Porchester Shipyard	19 July 1970
CUTLASS	P 274	Vosper Thornycroft Group, Porchester Shipyard	12 Nov 1970
SABRE	P 275	Vosper Thornycroft Group, Porchester Shipyard	5 Mar 1971

Displacement, tons: 102 full load
Dimensions, feet (metres): 90.0 wl;
100.0 oa × 26.6 × 6.4 (27.4; 30.5 × 8.1 × 1.9)
Main engines: 2 Rolls-Royce Proteus
gas-turbines = 40 knots (2 Foden diesels for
cruising in CODAG arrangement)
Range, miles: 425 at 35 knots; 1,500 at 11.5
knots

Complement: 12 (2 officers and 10 ratings)

When it became evident that the Soviet
"Osa" and "Komar" classes (1961-63) of
missile-armed fast attack craft posed a
major threat to the fleet the Ministry of
Defence decided to provide craft which
would provide training against such a threat.

Based on the design of the very successful
"Brave" class three craft were built, all
capable of shipping a third gas turbine and
a gun armament if required.

Cutlass △

▽ Sabre

Type: Fast Attack Craft – Patrol   *Class:* "Tenacity"

Name	No.	Builders	Commissioned
TENACITY	P 276	Vosper Thornycroft Ltd	17 Feb 1973

Displacement, tons: 165 standard;
220 full load
Dimensions, feet (metres):
144.5 oa × 26.6 × 7.8 (44.1 × 8.1 × 2.4)
Guns: 2 MGs
Main engines: 3 Rolls-Royce Proteus gas
turbines; 3 shafts; 12,750 bhp = 40 knots;

2 Paxman Ventura 6-cylinder diesels on
wing shafts for cruising = 16 knots
Range, miles: 2,500 at 15 knots
Complement: 32 (4 officers and 28 ratings)

This craft was built as a private venture at
Camber Shipyard Portsmouth. Although

capable of carrying missiles her armament
was cut to two machine-guns when she was
bought by the Ministry of Defence in
January 1972. Since her subsequent refit
she has been employed primarily on Fishery
Protection duties.

Tenacity

Type: Coastal Patrol Vessel   *Class:* Modified "Ton"

Name	No.	Builders	Commissioned
BEACHAMPTON	P 1007 (ex-M 1107	Goole SB Co	1953
MONKTON	P 1055 (ex-M 1155)	Herd & Mackenzie, Buckie	1956
WASPERTON	P 1089 (ex-M 1189)	J. Samuel White & Co Ltd	1956
WOLVERTON	P 1093 (ex-M 1193)	Montrose SY Co	1957
YARNTON	P 1096 (ex-M 1196)	Pickersgill	1956

Displacement, tons: 360 standard; 425 full
load
Dimensions, feet (metres): 140.0 pp;
153.0 oa × 28.8 × 8.2 (42.7; 46.3 × 8.8 × 2.5)
Guns: 2 × 40-mm Bofors (single, 1 forward,
1 aft)

Main engines: 2 diesels; 2 shafts;
3,000 bhp = 15 knots
Oil fuel, tons: 45
Range, miles: 2,300 at 13 knots
Complement: 30 (5 officers and 25 ratings,
but varies)

Remarks on this class are contained in the
section of the "Ton" class minesweepers.
Form 6th Patrol Squadron, Hong Kong.

Type: Seaward Defence Boats   *Class:* "Ford"

Name	No.	Builders	Commissioned
DEE (ex-*Beckford*)	P 3104	Wm. Simons, Renfrew	1953
DROXFORD	P 3113	Pimblott, Northwich	1954

Displacement, tons: 120 standard; 142 full
load
Dimensions, feet (metres): 110.0 wl;
117.2 oa × 20.0 × 7.0 (33.6; 35.7 × 6.1 × 2.1)
A/S weapons: DC rails; large and small DC
Main engines: Davey Paxman diesels.
Foden engine on centre shaft.
1,100 bhp = 18 knots
Oil fuel, tons: 23

Complement: 19

The alarms generated by the Korean War
and the coetaneous build-up of the Soviet
submarine fleet prompted the design of
these steel-hulled patrol craft fitted with a
small sonar. Although a number was
transferred to Ghana, Nigeria and South
Africa none has been tested under real war

conditions and the class is probably too
slow for such emergencies. A number was
employed off Singapore during Indonesian
Confrontation but now only two of the
original twenty remain in the Navy List – *Dee*
(ex-*Beckford*) attached to Liverpool
University RNU and *Droxford* with Glasgow
University RNU.

Survey Ships

Type: Survey Ship   Class: "Hecla"

Name	No.	Builders	Commissioned
HECLA	A 133	Yarrow & Co, Blythswood	9 Sept 1965
HECATE	A 137	Yarrow & Co Ltd, Scotstoun	20 Dec 1965
HYDRA	A 144	Yarrow & Co, Blythswood	5 May 1966

Displacement, tons: 1,915 light; 2,733 full load

Measurement, tons: 2,898 gross

Length, feet (metres): 235 (71.6) pp; 260.1 (79.3) oa

Beam, feet (metres): 49.1 (15.0)

Draught, feet (metres): 15.6 (4.7)

Aircraft: 1 Wasp helicopter

Main engines: Diesel-electric drive; 1 shaft; 3 Paxman "Ventura" 12-cylinder Vee turbocharged diesels; 3,840 bhp; 1 electric motor; 2,000 shp

Speed, knots: 14

Oil fuel, tons: 450

Range, miles: 20,000 at 9 knots

Complement: 118 (14 officers and 104 ratings)

Of the eleven surveying ships with which the Hydrographic Department started the war of 1939-45 only one, *Endeavour* had been built for survey duties and she in 1912. This policy was continued until 1950 when *Vidal*, designed for hydrographic work by the Director General of Ships, Admiralty, was laid down. She was the first survey ship to carry a helicopter and this was a facility built-in to the ships planned to replace the ex-frigates and minesweepers as they became due for paying-off. The recommendation that these ships should be of commercial design was not well received in the Admiralty but so they were and, with some attention to stability, they have proved very successful.

They are strengthened for ice-navigation and fitted with a bow-thruster, twin laboratories, a photographic studio, a helicopter hangar, Land-Rover garage, workshops, storerooms and comprehensive air-conditioning. The average cost was £1,250,000.

Hecla

Type: Survey Ship   Class: Improved "Hecla"

Name	No.	Builders	Commissioned
HERALD	A 138	Robb Caledon, Leith	31 Oct 1974

Displacement, tons: 2,000 standard; 2,945 full load

Dimensions, feet (metres): 260.1 oa × 49.1 × 15.6 (79.3 × 15 × 4.7)

Aircraft: 1 Wasp helicopter

Main engines: Diesel-electric drive; 1 shaft

Speed, knots: 14

Range, miles: 12,000 at 11 knots

Complement: 128

An improvement on the "Hecla" class and fitted with Hydroplot navigation system, computerised data logging, a gravimeter, magnetometer, coring and oceanographic winches and a bow thruster.

Herald

Coastal Survey Ships

Type: Coastal Survey Ship			Class: "Bulldog"
Name	**No.**	**Builders**	**Commissioned**
BULLDOG	A 317	Brooke Marine Ltd, Lowestoft	21 Mar 1968
BEAGLE	A 319	Brooke Marine Ltd, Lowestoft	9 May 1968
FOX	A 320	Brooke Marine Ltd, Lowestoft	11 July 1968
FAWN	A 325	Brooke Marine Ltd, Lowestoft	10 Sept 1968

Displacement, tons: 800 standard; 1,088 full load

Dimensions, feet (metres):
189 oa × 37.5 × 12 (60.1 × 11.4 × 3.6)

Main engines: 4 Lister Blackstone ERS8M, 8-cylinder, 4-stroke diesels, coupled to 2 shafts; cp propellers; 2,000 bhp = 15 knots

Range, miles: 4,000 at 12 knots

Complement: 38 (4 officers and 34 ratings)

In order to complement the "Hecla" class of deep-sea surveying ships with a class of coastal ships the commercially designed "Bulldog" class was ordered in 1965. The four ships are fitted with passive tank stabilisers, Decca Hi-Fix system and automatic steering. With the RNs withdrawal from foreign deployments the majority of the work done by these ships is now in Home Waters.

Bulldog

Inshore Survey Craft

Type: Inshore Survey Craft

Class: "E"

Name	No.	Builders	Commissioned
ECHO	A 70	J. Samuel White & Co Ltd, Cowes	12 Sept 1958
ENTERPRISE	A 71	M. W. Blackmore & Sons Ltd, Bideford	1959
EGERIA	A 72	Wm. Weatherhead & Sons, Cockenzie	1959

Displacement, tons: 120 standard; 160 full load

Dimensions, feet (metres):
106.8 oa × 22.0 × 6.8 (32.6 × 7 × 2.1)

Main engines: 2 Paxman diesels; 2 shafts; controllable pitch propellers;

1,400 bhp = 14 knots

Oil fuel, tons: 15

Range, miles: 1,600 at 10 knots

Complement: 18 (2 officers and 16 ratings); accommodation for 22 (4 officers and 18 ratings)

Built for surveying in close waters such as harbour approaches and estuaries these craft are fitted with two echo-sounders, sonar, radar, wire-sweeping gear and a small surveying motor-boat.

Enterprise

Type: Modified Inshore Minesweepers

Class: "Ham"

Name	No.	Builders	Commissioned
WATERWITCH (ex-Powderham)	M 272	J. Samuel White & Co Ltd, Cowes	1959
WOODLARK (ex-Yaxham)	M 2780	J. Samuel White & Co Ltd, Cowes	1958

Displacement, tons: 120 standard; 160 full load

Dimensions, feet (metres):
107.5 oa × 22 × 5.5 (32.4 × 6.5 × 1.7)

Main engines: Diesels; 2 shafts;

1,100 bhp = 14 knots

Range, miles: 1,500 at 12 knots

Complement: 18 (2 officers and 16 ratings)

These craft are employed on similar duties

as Echo and her sisters, having been converted in the late 1960s to replace the surveying launches Meda and Medusa. Waterwitch is operated by the RMAS.

Waterwitch

Auxiliary Services

Type: Large Fleet Tanker (AOF(L))   Class: "Ol"

Name	No.	Builders	Commissioned
OLWEN (ex-*Olynthus*)*	A 122	Hawthorn Leslie, Hebburn	21 June 1965
OLNA	A 123	Hawthorn Leslie, Hebburn	1 April 1966
OLMEDA (ex-*Oleander*)	A 124	Swan Hunter, Wallsend	18 Oct 1965

*Refit

Displacement, tons: 10,890 light; 36,000 full load
Measurement, tons: 25,100 deadweight; 18,600 gross
Dimensions, feet (metres): 611.1 pp; 648.0 oa × 84.0 × 34.0 (185.9; 197.5 × 25.6 × 10.5)
Aircraft: 2 Wessex helicopters (can carry 3)
Main engines: Pametrada double reduction geared-turbines; 26,500 shp = 19 knots

Boilers: 2 Babcock & Wilcox (750 psi; 950°F)
Complement: 87 (25 officers and 62 ratings)

These were the largest and fastest ships in the Royal Fleet Auxiliary when completed in 1965-66. They can replenish the entire fleet by all means including vertrep (by helicopter). They are fully air-conditioned and strengthened for operations in ice. *Olna* is fitted with a bow-thruster.

The original capacity was listed as 18,400 tons FFO, 1,720 tons diesel, 130 tons lub-oil, 3,730 tons Avcat and 280 tons Mogas.

The hangar is split with accommodation for three Wessex helicopters to port and vehicles to starboard.

Olwen △

▽ Olna

Type: Large Fleet Tanker (AOF(L))   *Class:* Later "Tide"

Name	No.	Builders	Commissioned
TIDESPRING	A 75	Hawthorn Leslie, Hebburn	18 Jan 1963
TIDEPOOL	A 76	Hawthorn Leslie, Hebburn	28 June 1963

Displacement, tons: 8,531 light; 27,400 full load

Measurement, tons: 18,900 deadweight; 14,130 gross

Dimensions, feet (metres): 550.0 pp; 583.0 oa × 71.0 × 32.0

(167.7; 177.6 × 21.6 × 9.8)

Main engines: Double reduction geared turbines; 15,000 shp = 18.3 knots

Boilers: 2 Babcock & Wilcox

Complement: 110 (30 Officers and 80 ratings)

Predecessors of the "Ol" class these ships have the same hangar arrangements as those ships but carry only 13,000 tons FFO. Both launched in 1962.

Tidespring

Type: Small Fleet Tanker (AOF(S))   *Class:* "Rover"

Name	No.	Builders	Commissioned
GREEN ROVER	A 268	Swan Hunter, Hebburn-on-Tyne	15 Aug 1969
GREY ROVER	A 269	Swan Hunter, Hebburn-on-Tyne	10 April 1970
BLUE ROVER	A 270	Swan Hunter, Hebburn-on-Tyne	15 July 1970
GOLD ROVER	A 271	Swan Hunter, Wallsend-on-Tyne	22 Mar 1974
BLACK ROVER	A 273	Swan Hunter, Wallsend-on-Tyne	23 Aug 1974

Displacement, tons: 4,700 light; 11,522 full load

Measurement, tons: 6,692 (A 271 and 273), 6,822 remainder deadweight; 7,510 gross; 3,185 net

Dimensions, feet (metres): 461.0 oa × 63.0 × 24.0 (140.6 × 19.2 × 7.3)

Main engines: 2 Pielstick 16-cylinder diesels; 1 shaft; controllable pitch propeller; 15,300 bhp — 18 knots

Range, miles: 15,000 at 15 knots

Complement: 47 (16 officers and 31 men)

This class of unusual appearance have their funnel and bridge about a third of their length from the stern to provide space for a helicopter deck. A goods lift gives access to this deck from the stores. Cargo capacity is 6,600 tons of fuel.

In addition to the controllable pitch propeller a bow-thruster is fitted to facilitate berthing.

The last ship, *Black Rover*, cost £7,000,000, an increase of £4,000,000 over the price of the first of class.

Gold Rover

Gold Rover △

Black Rover

Type: Support Tanker (AOS)   *Class:* "Orangeleaf"

Name	No.	Builders	Commissioned
ORANGELEAF (ex-MV *Southern Satellite*)	A 80	Furness Shipbuilding Co Ltd, Haverton Hill on Tees	June 1965

Measurement, tons: 18,222 deadweight; 12,146 gross; 6,800 net
Dimensions, feet (metres): 525 pp; 556.5 oa × 71.7 × 30.5 (160.1; 169.7 × 21.9 × 9.3)

Main engines: Doxford 6-cylinder diesel; 6,800 bhp = 14 knots
Oil fuel, tons: 1,610
Complement: 35

Originally built for South Georgia Co. Ltd, as MB *Southern Satellite* she was chartered by the Admiralty on 25 May 1959. Fitted for fuelling abeam and astern. Due to be returned to owners late 1978.

Orangeleaf

Type: Support Tanker (AOS)   *Class:* "Cherryleaf"

Name	No.	Builders	Commissioned
CHERRYLEAF	A 82	Rheinstahl Nordseewerke	1963
(ex-*Overseas Adventurer*)			

Measurement, tons: 19,700 deadweight; 13,700 gross, 7,648 net
Dimensions, feet (metres): 559 × 72 × 30 (170.5 × 22 × 9.2)
Machinery: 7-cylinder MAN diesel, 8,400 bhp = 16 knots

Complement: 55

An older *Cherryleaf* was returned to her original owners, Molasses and General Transport Co, in 1966. Her successor completed in Germany as *Overseas*

Adventurer in 1963 was chartered for the Royal Fleet Auxiliary in March 1973 and renamed. She has no replenishment-at-sea capability.

Cherryleaf

Type: Support Tanker (AOS)   *Class:* "Plumleaf"

Name	No.	Builders	Commissioned
PLUMLEAF	A 78	Blyth DD & Eng Co Ltd	July 1960

Displacement, tons: 26,480 full load
Measurement, tons: 19,430 deadweight; 12,459 gross
Dimensions, feet (metres): 534 pp;

560 oa × 72 × 30 (162.9; 170.8 × 22 × 9.2)
Main engines: N.E. Doxford 6-cylinder diesels; 9,500 bhp = 15.5 knots
Complement: 55

Launched on 29 March 1960. She can carry out replenishment both abeam and astern.

Plumleaf

Type: Support Tanker (AOS)　　　　　　　　　　　　　　　　　　　　　　　　*Class:* "Pearleaf"

Name	No.	Builders	Commissioned
PEARLEAF	A 77	Blythswood Shipbuilding Co Ltd, Scotstoun	Jan 1960

Displacement, tons: 25,790 full load
Measurement, tons: 18,711 deadweight; 12,353 gross; 7,215 net
Dimensions, feet (metres): 535 pp; 568 oa × 71.7 × 30

(162.7; 173.2 × 21.9 × 9.2)
Main engines: Rowan Doxford 6-cylinder diesels; 8,800 bhp = 16 knots
Complement: 55

She was launched on 15 October 1959 and chartered from her owners Jacobs and Partners Ltd, on completion. She is fitted for fuelling abeam and astern.

Pearleaf △▽

Type: Coastal Tanker (AO(H)) — *Class:* "Eddy"

Name	No.	Builders	Commissioned
EDDYFIRTH	A 261	Lobnitz & Co Ltd, Renfrew	10 Feb 1954

Displacement, tons: 1,960 light; 4,160 full load
Measurement, tons: 2,200 deadweight; 2,222 gross
Dimensions, feet (metres): 270 pp; 286 oa × 44 × 17.2 (82.4; 87.2 × 13.4 × 5.2)

Main engines: 1 set triple expansion; 1 shaft; 1,750 ihp = 12 knots
Boilers: 2 oil-burning cylindrical

The sole survivor of a class of eight ships built in the early 1950s. *Eddybay,*

Eddybeach, Eddycliff, Eddycreek and *Eddyreef* were deleted in 1963-64, *Eddyrock* in 1967 and *Eddyness* in 1970. She has a cargo capacity of 1,650 tons.

Eddyfirth

Type: Fleet Replenishment Ship (AEFS) — *Class:* "Fort"

Name	No.	Builders	Commissioned
FORT GRANGE	A 385	Scott-Lithgow	1978
FORT AUSTIN	A 386	Scott-Lithgow	1979

Displacement, tons: 20,000
Measurement, tons: 9,843 deadweight
Dimensions, feet (metres): 603 × 79 × 29.5 (183.9 × 24.1 × 9)
Aircraft: 1 Wessex helicopter
Main engines: 1 8-cylinder Sulzer diesel;

23,300 hp; single screw = 20 knots

Ordered in November 1971 these two ships will provide up-to-date replenishment facilities with a helicopter hangar and a fuelling point for force A/S helicopters. A/S

stores for helicopters are also carried on board. *Fort Grange* was laid down 9 November 1973 and launched 9 December 1976. *Fort Austin* was laid down 9 December 1975 and launched 8 March 1978.

Type: Fleet Replenishment Ships (AEFS) — *Class:* "Resource"

Name	No.	Builders	Commissioned
RESOURCE	A 480	Scotts Shipbuilding & Eng Co, Greenock	16 May 1967
REGENT	A 486	Harland & Wolff, Belfast	6 June 1967

Displacement, tons: 22,890 full load
Measurement, tons: 18,029 gross
Dimensions, feet (metres): 600.0 pp; 640 oa × 77.2 × 26.1 (182.8; 195.1 × 23.5 × 8)
Aircraft: 1 Wessex helicopter
Guns: Fitted for 2 × 40-mm Bofors (single) which are not carried in peacetime

Main engines: AEI steam turbines; 20,000 shp = 21 knots
Complement: 119 R.F.A. officers and ratings; 52 Naval Dept industrial and non-industrial civil servants; 11 Royal Navy (1 officer and 10 ratings) for helicopter flying and maintenance

Both ordered on 24 January 1963, they were the first RFA ships designed specifically as Fleet Replenishment Ships, their predecessors having been converted merchant ships. They carry ammunition, explosives, food and naval stores for replenishing the fleet at sea by jackstay or helicopter.

Regent

Type: Armament Support Ship (AE)

Class: "Retainer"

Name	No.	Builders	Commissioned
RESURGENT (ex-*Changchow*)	A 280	Scotts Shipbuilding & Engineering Co Ltd, Greenock	1951
RETAINER (ex-*Chungking*)	A 329	Scotts Shipbuilding & Engineering Co Ltd, Greenock	1950

Displacement, tons: 14,400
Measurement, tons: *Resurgent* 9,357;
Retainer 9,498 gross
Dimensions, feet (metres):
477.2 oa × 62 × 29 (145.8 × 18.9 × 8.8)
Main engines: Doxford diesels; 1 shaft;
6,500 bhp = 16 knots

Oil fuel, tons: 925
Complement: 107

An unmistakable pair of ships which were originally built for the China Navigation Company. *Retainer* started her career on the China coast and was bought by the

Admiralty in 1952, being converted by Palmers, Hebburn Co Ltd, for naval service in 1954-55. The same firm carried out further conversion work in 1957, providing lifts and additional storage. *Resurgent* was taken over on completion. Both have a helicopter platform aft. To be replaced by "Fort" class.

Resurgent

Type: Stores Support Ship (AVS/AFS)   *Class:* "Ness"

Name	No.	Builders	Commissioned
LYNESS	A 339	Swan Hunter & Wigham Richardson Ltd, Wallsend-on-Tyne	22 Dec 1966
STROMNESS	A 344	Swan Hunter & Wigham Richardson Ltd, Wallsend-on-Tyne	21 Mar 1967
TARBATNESS	A 345	Swan Hunter & Wigham Richardson Ltd, Wallsend-on-Tyne	10 Aug 1967

Displacement, tons: 9,010 light; 16,792 full load

Measurement, tons: 7,782 deadweight; 12,359 gross; 4,744 net

Dimensions, feet (metres): 490 pp; 524 oa × 72 × 22.0 (149.4; 159.7 × 22 × 6.7)

Aircraft: Helicopter deck

Main engines: Wallsend-Sulzer 8-cylinder RD.76 diesel; 11,520 bhp = 18 knots

Complement: 151 (25 officers, 82 ratings, 44 stores personnel)

All were ordered on 7 December 1964 to a new Admiralty design – *Lyness* was completed as an Air Stores Support Ship, her sisters as Stores Support Ships. Cargo handling is monitored by closed-circuit television and facilitated by lifts and new replenishment gear. Working and living spaces are air-conditioned. *Lyness* cost £3,500,000.

Stromness △

▽ Tarbatness

Type: Armament Store Carrier (AKF)   Class: "Throsk"

Name	No.	Builders	Commissioned
THROSK	A 379	Cleland SB Co, Wallsend	Sept 1977

Displacement, tons: 1,968 full-load
Measurement, tons: 1,150 deadweight
Dimensions, feet (metres): 210.9 × 39 × 15 (64.3 × 11.9 × 4.6)

Main engines: 2 Mirrlees-Blackstone diesels; 3,000 bhp; 1 shaft = 14 knots
Range, miles: 5,000 at 10 knots
Complement: 22 (plus 10 spare bunks)

Ordered in December 1975 this ship has two holds for armament stores and is fitted with two 5 tonne derricks. With a flush deck she has now replaced *Robert Middleton*.

Type: Store Carrier (AK)   Class: "Hebe"

Name	No.	Builders	Commissioned
BACCHUS	A 404	Henry Robb Ltd, Leith	Sept 1962
HEBE	A 406	Henry Robb Ltd, Leith	May 1962

Displacement, tons: 2,740 light; 8,173 full load
Measurement, tons: 5,312 deadweight; 4,823 gross; 2,441 net
Dimensions, feet (metres): 379 oa × 55 × 22 (115.6 × 16.8 × 6.4)

Main engines: Swan Hunter Sulzer diesel; 1 shaft; 5,500 bhp = 15 knots
Oil fuel, tons: 720
Complement: 57

These two well-known ships were originally built for the British India Steam Navigation Co. Ltd, as dry-cargo ships and chartered by the Admiralty on completion. In 1973 both were bought by the P and O S.N. Co, remaining on charter. Their task is the ferrying of stores to various naval bases.

Bacchus

Type: Mooring, Salvage & Boom Vessel   Class: "Wild Duck" "Improved Wild Duck" "Later Wild Duck"

Name		No.	Builders	Commissioned
MANDARIN	}A	P 192	Cammell Laird & Co Ltd, Birkenhead	5 Mar 1964
PINTAIL		P 193	Cammell Laird & Co Ltd, Birkenhead	Mar 1964
GARGANEY	}B	P 194	Brooke Marine Ltd, Lowestoft	20 Sept 1966
GOLDENEYE		P 195	Brooke Marine Ltd, Lowestoft	21 Dec 1966
GOOSANDER	}C	P 196	Robb Caledon Ltd	10 Sept 1973
POCHARD		P 197	Robb Caledon Ltd	11 Dec 1973

Displacement, tons: 950 standard; 1,125 full load (*Goosander* and *Pochard*)
Dimensions, feet (metres): 197.6 (60.2) (*Goosander* and *Pochard*); 189.8 (57.9) (*Garganey* and *Goldeneye*); 181.8 (55.4) including horns (*Mandarin* and *Pintail*) × 40.1 × 13.8 (12.2 × 4.2)
Main engines: 1 Davey Paxman 16-cylinder

diesel; 1 shaft, controllable pitch propeller; 550 bhp = 10 knots
Range, miles: 3,000 at 10.2 knots; 750 bhp; 10 knots (*Goosander* and *Pochard*)
Complement: 26

Mandarin was the first of a new class of marine service vessels and was launched

on 17 September 1963. Her sister is *Pintail*, the other four ships being in two pairs varying marginally from the original two. All combine the ability to carry out the three main tasks listed in their type name. Can carry out tidal lifts of 260 tons over the apron.

Goosander

Type: Mooring, Salvage and Boom Vessel | | | *Class:* "Kin"

Name	No.	Builders	Commissioned
KINGARTH	A 232	A. Hall, Aberdeen	1944
KINBRACE	A 281	A. Hall, Aberdeen	1945
KINLOSS	A 482	A. Hall, Aberdeen	1945
UPLIFTER	A 507	Smith's Dock Co Ltd	1944

Displacement, tons: 950 standard; 1,050 full load
Measurement, tons: 262 deadweight, 775 gross
Dimensions, feet (metres): 179.2 oa × 35.2 × 12.0 (54 × 10.6 × 3.6)
Main engines: 1 British Polar Atlas M44M diesel; 630 bhp = 9 knots
Complement: 34

Originally a class of eight built during World War II. The four surviving ships were re-engined – *Kinloss* in 1963-64, the remainder in 1966-67 – their original triple-expansion reciprocating machinery being replaced by Polar diesels. Until 1971 the class was classified as Coastal Salvage Vessels, all being equipped with lifting horns capable of raising 200 tons

deadweight. In the 1950s *Kingarth* was on charter to the Royal Hellenic Navy and *Dispenser* (deleted in 1975) was on charter to the Liverpool and Glasgow Salvage Association until 1971. *Succour, Swin* and *Lifeline* also deleted.

Type: Mooring, Salvage and Boom Vessel | | | *Class:* "Lay"

Name	No.	Builders	Commissioned
LAYMOOR (RN)	P 190	Wm. Simons & Co Ltd (Simons-Lobnitz Ltd)	9 Dec 1959
LAYBURN	P 191	Wm. Simons & Co Ltd (Simons-Lobnitz Ltd)	7 June 1960

Displacement, tons: 800 standard; 1,050 full load
Dimensions, feet (metres): 192.7 oa × 34.5 × 11.5 (59 × 10.3 × 3.4)
Main engines: Triple expansion; 1 shaft; 1,300 ihp = 10 knots
Boilers: 2 Foster Wheeler "D" type; 200 psi
Complement: 26 (4 officers and 22 ratings)

These two ships were the first post-war designed MSBVs and have remained the only pair of the class to be built. They were designed to incorporate the three tasks included in their classification, being able to handle all sizes of mooring and navigational buoys, carry out light salvage work and lay and operate all forms of booms and nets.

They replaced the older classes of boom vessels of the "Moor" class (17 ships) and the "Bar" class (71 ships) which were built from 1938 and throughout the war and were in their turn succeeded by the "Wild Ducks". They were fitted for both RN and civilian manning, *Laymoor* currently being under the White Ensign.

Type: Coastal Tanker   *Class:* "Oilpress"

Name	No.	Builders	Commissioned
OILPRESS	Y 21	Appledore Shipbuilders Ltd	1969
OILSTONE	Y 22	Appledore Shipbuilders Ltd	1969
OILWELL	Y 23	Appledore Shipbuilders Ltd	1969
OILFIELD	Y 24	Appledore Shipbuilders Ltd	1969
OILBIRD	Y 25	Appledore Shipbuilders Ltd	1969
OILMAN	Y 26	Appledore Shipbuilders Ltd	1969

Displacement, tons: 280 standard; 530 full load

Dimensions, feet (metres): 130.0 wl; 139.5 oa × 30.0 × 8.3 (39.6; 41.5 × 9 × 2.5)

Main engines: 1 Lister Blackstone ES6 diesel; 1 shaft; 405 shp at 900 rpm

Complement: 11 (4 officers and 7 ratings)

Originally designed as coastal tankers these six ships are now operated as yard tankers.

Three are diesel carriers and three transport FFO. First six were ordered on 10 May 1967 and *Waterman* in June 1977, being launched 24 November 1977..

Oilpress △   ▽ Oilstone

Type: Trials Ship   *Class:* "Newton"

Name	No.	Builders	Commissioned
NEWTON	A 367	Scott Lithgow Ltd	17 June 1976

Displacement, tons: 3,940 full load

Dimensions, feet (metres): 323.5 × 53 × 18.5 (98.6 × 16 × 5.7)

Main engines: Diesel electric; 3 Mirrlees Blackstone diesels; 1 shaft; 4,350 bhp = 15 knots

Range, miles: 5,000 at 13 knots

Complement: 61 (including 12 scientists)

Although ordered in November 1971 she was not laid down until 19 December 1973 and was eventually launched on

25 June 1975. She is designed to carry out sonar propagation trials and can also act as a cable-layer, being fitted with large cable tanks. Her propulsion system is very quiet and she is fitted with a bow-thruster as well as Kort nozzle.

Newton

Type: Trials Ship

Class: "Whitehead"

Name	No.	Builders	Commissioned
WHITEHEAD	A 364	Scotts Shipbuilding Co Ltd, Greenock	1971

Displacement, tons: 3,040 full load
Dimensions, feet (metres): 291.0 wl;
319.0 oa × 48.0 × 17.0
(88.8; 97.3 × 14.6 × 5.2)
Main engines: 2 Paxman 12 YLCM diesels;
1 shaft; 3,400 bhp = 15.5 knots
Range, miles: 4,000 at 12 knots

Complement: 10 officers, 32 ratings,
15 trials and scientific staff

Whitehead is primarily designed for the
underwater launch of weapons and research
systems. She is fitted to prepare such
material and not only does she have firing

and control circuits for a number of weapon
systems but also mounts tracking and
analysing equipment. Launched on
5 May 1970 she is named after Robert
Whitehad, the pioneer of torpedo design.

Whitehead

Type: Trials Ship

Class: "Crystal"

Name	No.	Builders	Commissioned
CRYSTAL	RDV 01	HM Dockyard, Devonport	30 Nov 1971

Displacement, tons: 3,040
Dimensions, feet (metres):
413.5 × 56.0 × 5.5 (126.1 × 17.1 × 1.7)
Complement: 60, including scientists

This bizarre looking floating platform was
built to provide a platform for acoustic and
research projects at Portland. She has no
means of propulsion or steering and is a

harbour-based craft attached to the
Admiralty Underwater Weapons
Establishment. She is under Dockyard
Control.

Crystal

Type: Trials Ship			*Class:* "Miner"
Name	No.	Builders	Commissioned
BRITANNIC (ex-*Miner V*)	—	Philip & Son Ltd, Dartmouth	26 June 1941
STEADY (ex-*Miner VII*)	—	Philip & Son Ltd, Dartmouth	31 Mar 1944

Displacement, tons: 300 standard; 355 full load
Dimensions, feet (metres):
110.2 × 26.5 × 8.0 (33.6 × 8.1 × 2.4)
Main engines: Ruston & Hornsby diesels;
2 shafts; 360 bhp = 10 knots

The original eight ships of this class were built during World War II as controlled minelayers. Since 1945 they were used for a number of tasks including submarine support. *Miner V* was converted into a harbour cable-layer and renamed *Britannic* in 1960 while *Miner VII* was adapted as a stabilisation trials ship and renamed *Steady* in the same year. *Britannic* is now laid up at Portland, *Steady* operates off the Channel Islands while the remaining six ships including *Miner III,* which finished her life as a diving tender at Pembroke, have been deleted.

Britannic

Type: Torpedo Recovery Vessel

Class: "Torrent"

Name	No.	Builders	Commissioned
TORRENT	A 127	Cleland SB Co, Wallsend	10 Sept 1971
TORRID	A 128	Cleland SB Co, Wallsend	Jan 1972

Measurement, tons: 550 gross
Dimensions, feet (metres):
151.0 × 31.5 × 11 (46.1 × 9.6 × 3.4)
Main engines: Paxman diesels;
700 bhp = 12 knots
Complement: 19

When the need for new torpedo recovery vessels became acute in the early 1960s six "Ham" class inshore minesweepers and a store carrier were converted for this task. The larger and custom-built ships of the "Torrent" class followed in 1971-72. They are more capable of recovery in heavy weather and can carry twenty-two torpedoes in their holds and ten on deck. The torpedoes are recovered over a stern ramp as first used in the "Hams".

Four new TRVs were ordered in 1977 from Hall Russell, Aberdeen.

Torrid △

▽ Thomas Grant

Type: Torpedo Recovery Vessel

Class: "Thomas Grant"

Name	No.	Builders	Commissioned
THOMAS GRANT	—	Charles Hill & Sons Ltd, Bristol	July 1953

Displacement, tons: 209 light; 461 full load
Measurement, tons: 252 deadweight;
218 gross
Dimensions, feet (metres):
113.5 × 25.5 × 8.8 (34.6 × 7.8 × 2.7)
Main engines: 2 diesels; Speed = 9 knots

Originally built as a store-carrier she was converted into a TRV in 1968.

Type: Torpedo Recovery Vessel

Class: "Ham"

Name
BUCKLESHAM M 2614
DOWNHAM M 2622
EVERINGHAM M 2626
FRITHAM M 2630
HAVERSHAM M 2635
LASHAM M 2636

Displacement, tons: 120 standard; 159 full load
Dimensions, feet (metres): 2601 Series: 100 pp; 106.5 oa × 21.2 × 5.5 (30.5; 32.4 × 6.5 × 1.7); 2793 Series: 100 pp; 107.5 oa × 22 × 5.8 (30.5; 32.1 × 6.6 × 1.8)
Main engines: 2 Paxman diesels;

1,100 bhp = 14 knots
Oil fuel, tons: 15
Complement: 15 (2 officers and 13 ratings)

In the early 1960s it was planned to scrap a number of the "Ham" class Inshore Minesweepers which were only a few years

out of the building yard. A proposal for converting a number of these vessels for other purposes was accepted in 1962 and this plan included six for torpedo recovery duties. A stern ramp was fitted and these craft remain a useful addition to the fleet.

Type: Torpedo Recovery Vessel

Class: "TRV 72 Type"

Name
ENDEAVOUR

A number of this type of TRV, based on the wartime Air Sea Rescue hull, are still in service. 72 operates in the Clyde area.

Displacement, tons: 88

Dimensions, feet (metres): 76 × 14.5 × 9.8 (23.2 × 4.4 × 3)
Main engines: 1 Lister-Blackstone diesel; 337 hp; 1 shaft = 10.5 knots

Endeavour was built for Liverpool Customs by H. Dunston & Co in 1966. Subsequently bought by MoD. Operates as TRV and range safety craft at Bincleaves Torpedo Range, Portland.

Type: Experimental Ship

Class: "LCT"

Name
WHIMBREL (ex-NSC (E) 1012) A 179

Displacement, tons: 300
Dimensions, feet (metres): 187 × 29.5 × 5 (57 × 9 × 1.5)
Main engines: Diesels; 2 shafts

Originally one of the very numerous class of LCT(3)s she was converted for research duties as NSC(E)1012. She was subsequently renamed and is employed by the Underwater Weapons Establishment,

Portland. She is the sole survivor of an era of research ships which included *Icewhale* of 290 tons and *Sarepta* (ex-German *Frieda Peters*) of 470 tons both of which were paid off in the early 1970s.

Whimbrel

Type: Cable Ship   *Class:* "Bull"

Name	No.	Builders	Commissioned
ST. MARGARETS	A 259	Swan Hunter & Wigham Richardson Ltd	1944

Displacement, tons: 1,300 light; 2,500 full load
Measurement, tons: 1,524 gross; 1,200 deadweight
Dimensions, feet (metres): 228.8 pp; 252 oa × 36.5 × 16.3 (76 × 10.9 × 4.8)

Main engines: Triple expansion; 2 shafts; 1,250 ihp = 12 knots

This ship was one of a class of four built during World War II. *Bullfrog* and *Bullhead* were transferred to Cable and Wireless in

1947 while *Bullfinch* was paid off in 1975 remaining in reserve at Plymouth. Operated by RMAS *St Margarets* is still fitted to carry a 4-inch gun and 4 × 20-mm guns although no armament is carriedB

Type: Target Ship   *Class:* "Swedish"

Name
WAKEFUL (ex-*Dan*, ex-*Heracles* A 236

Displacement, tons: 900 full load
Gross tonnage: 492.6
Dimensions, feet (metres): 127.5 oa × 34.5 × 15.5 (38.9 × 10.7 × 4.7)
Main engines: 2 Ruston 9ATCM Mk 1A diesels; 4,750 bhp (212 revs); 1 shaft (4-bladed KaMeWa cp propeller)
Complement: 27 (5 officers, 22 ratings)

Built as a tug by Cochrane, Selby, Yorkshire. Purchased from Sweden in 1974 for £6,000 to act as Submarine Support Ship in the Clyde. "Navalised" during a £1,600,000 refit at Chatham in 1976 and transferred to Fishery Protection duties pending the commissioning of the "Island" class. Now working in the Clyde. She retains her towing

capability (Bollard pull, 50 tons) and has a limited salvage capability. She is the only ship in the RN with an ice-breaking ability and, as *Herakles*, was registered "Ice Class I" at Lloyds.

Type: Armament Carrier   *Class:* "Kinterbury"

Name	No.	Builders	Commissioned
KINTERBURY	A 378	Philip & Son Ltd	4 Mar 1943

Displacement, tons: 1,490 standard; 1,770 full load
Measurement, tons: 600 deadweight
Dimensions, feet (metres): 199.8 × 34.3 × 13 (60.9 × 10.2 × 4)

Main engines: Triple expansion; 1 shaft; 900 ihp = 11 knots
Coal, tons: 154

Launched in November 1942 and classified

as naval armament carrier. Converted in 1959 with hold stowage and derrick for handling guided missiles for *Girdle Ness*. Sister ship *Throsk* deleted in 1977).

Type: Armament Carrier   *Class:* "Maxim"

Name	No.	Builders	Commissioned
MAXIM	A 377	Lobnitz & Co Ltd, Renfrew	1945

Displacement, tons: 604
Measurement, tons: 340 deadweight
Dimensions, feet (metres): 144.5 × 25 × 8 (44.1 × 7.6 × 2.3)
Main engines: Reciprocating; 500 ihp = 9 knots

Complement: 13

Last of a class of six – launched 6 August 1945. *Chaltenden* became a dumb lighter in 1961 – *Snider*, *Gatling* and *Enfield* deleted 1968-70, *Nordenfeld* deleted 1975.

A group of smaller armament carriers are still represented by *Catapult*, *Flintlock* and *Howitzer*. Of these *Ballista*, *Blowpipe*, *Bowstring*, *Matchlock*, *Obus* and *Spear* have been deleted, the last (*Bowstring*) in 1975.

Type: Water Carrier   *Class:* "Water"

Name	No.	Builders	Commissioned
WATERCOURSE	Y 15	Drypool Engineering & Drydock Co, Hull	1974
WATERFOWL	Y 16	Drypool Engineering & Drydock Co, Hull	25 May 1974
WATERFALL	Y 17	Drypool Engineering & Drydock Co, Hull	1967
WATERSHED	Y 18	Drypool Engineering & Drydock Co, Hull	1967
WATERSPOUT	Y 19	Drypool Engineering & Drydock Co, Hull	1967
WATERSIDE	Y 20	Drypool Engineering & Drydock Co, Hull	1968
WATERMAN	—	R. Dunston (Hessle) Ltd	1979

Measurement, tons: 285 gross
Dimensions, feet (metres): 131.5 oa × 24.8 × 8 (40.1 × 7.5 × 2.3)
Main engines: 1 Diesel; 1 shaft; 600 bhp = 11 knots

Complement: 11

Harbour water carriers of which the first four were launched in 1966-67. The next pair, launched in 1973, have the after deck-house

extended forward. *Waterman* ordered in June 1977 and launched 24 November 1977.

Waterfall △

▽ Watershed

Type: Water Carrier

Class: "Spa"

Name	No.	Builders	Commissioned
SPAPOOL	A 222	Charles Hill & Sons Ltd, Bristol	1947

Displacement, tons: 1,219 full load
Measurement, tons: 630 deadweight; 719 gross
Dimensions, feet (metres): 172 oa × 30 × 12 (52.5 × 9.2 × 3.6)
Main engines: Triple expansion;

675 ihp = 9 knots
Coal, tons: 90

Originally a class of six water carriers built between 1944 and 1947. *Spabeck* was used as a tanker for High Test Peroxide for the

experimental submarines *Explorer* and *Excalibur* being disposed of in May 1966. *Spa* was deleted in 1970, *Spalake* and *Spaburn* in 1976 and *Spabrook* in 1977. All originally carried 1 × 3-inch gun and 2 × 20-mm guns.

Type: Water Carrier

Class: "Fresh"

Name
FRESHBURN
FRESHLAKE
FRESHSPRING

Displacement, tons: 594
Dimensions, feet (metres): 126.2 × 25.5 × 10.8 (38.5 × 7.8 × 3.3)
Main engines: Triple expansion; 450 ihp = 9 knots

Last of a wartime class of fourteen ships originally armed with 2 × 20-mm guns. *Freshbrook* and *Freshnet* deleted in 1963, *Freshwater* and *Freshwell* in 1968, *Freshford*, *Freshspray* and *Freshtarn* in

1969, *Freshener* in 1971, *Freshmere* in 1975 and *Freshpool* and *Freshpond* in 1976. *Freshspring* converted from coal to oil in 1961.

Type: Ocean Tug

Name	No.	Builders	Commissioned
ROYSTERER	A 361	Charles D. Holmes, Beverley Shipyard, Hull	26 April 1972
ROLLICKER	A 502	Charles D. Holmes, Beverley Shipyard, Hull	Feb 1973
ROBUST	—	Charles D. Holmes, Beverley Shipyard, Hull	6 April 1974

Displacement, tons: 1,630 full load
Dimensions, feet (metres): 162.0 pp; 179.7 oa × 38.5 × 18.0 (54 × 11.6 × 5.5)
Main engines: 2 Mirrlees KMR 6 diesels (by Lister Blackstone Mirrlees Marine Ltd.);

2 shafts; 4,500 bhp at 525 rpm = 15 knots
Range, miles: 13,000 at 12 knots
Complement: 31 (10 officers and 21 ratings) (and able to carry salvage party of 10 RN officers and ratings)

The largest and most powerful tugs ever built for the RN. Although designed for deep-sea towage and salvage work they are often used in harbours. They cost well over £2,000,000 apiece. Bollard pull – 50 tons.

Roysterer △▽

Type: Ocean Tug   *Class:* "Typhoon"

Name	No.	Builders	Commissioned
TYPHOON	A 95	Henry Robb & Co Ltd, Leith	1960

Displacement, tons: 800 standard; 1,380 full load
Dimensions, feet (metres):
200.0 oa × 40.0 × 13.0 (60.5 × 12 × 4)

Main engines: 2 turbocharged Vee type 12-cylinder diesels; 1 shaft; 2,750 bhp = over 16 knots

A "one-off" ship peculiar in having her twin diesels geared to a single shaft. She is fitted for salvage, fire-fighting and rescue work. Launched on 15 October 1958.

Typhoon △

▽ Agile

Type: Ocean Tug   *Class:* "Confiance"

Name	No.	Builders	Commissioned
AGILE	A 88	Goole SB Co	July 1959
ADVICE	A 89	A. & J. Inglis Ltd, Glasgow	Oct 1959
ACCORD	A 90	A. & J. Inglis Ltd, Glasgow	Sept 1958
CONFIANCE	A 289	A. & J. Inglis Ltd, Glasgow	27 Mar 1956
CONFIDENT	A 290	A. & J. Inglis Ltd, Glasgow	Jan 1956

Displacement, tons: 760 full load
Dimensions, feet (metres): 140.0 pp;
154.8 oa × 35.0 × 11.0
(42.7; 47.2 × 10.7 × 3.4)
Main engines: 4 Paxman HAXM diesels;

2 shafts (cp propellers);
1,800 bhp = 13 knots
Complement: 29 plus 13 salvage party

The three "A" named tugs, formerly rated as

dockyard tugs, were added to the
"Confiance" class in 1971. All fitted for
1 × 40-mm gun. It is unfortunate that the
word Confiance is not carried in the normal
dictionary.

Type: Ocean Tug   *Class:* "Samson"

Name	No.	Builders	Commissioned
SEA GIANT	A 288	Alexander Hall & Co Ltd, Aberdeen	1955
SUPERMAN	—	Alexander Hall & Co Ltd, Aberdeen	1954

Displacement, tons: 1,200 full load
Measurement, tons: 850 grosss
Dimensions, feet (metres):
180 oa × 37 × 14 (54 × 11.2 × 4.3)

Main engines: Triple expansion; 2 shafts;
3,000 ihp = 15 knots
Complement: 30

Launched 1953-54. *Superman* laid up at
Devonport. *Samson* sold commercially in
1977.

Sea Giant

Type: Ocean Tug   *Class:* "Bustler"

Name	No.	Builders	Commissioned
CYCLONE (ex-Growler)	A 111	Henry Robb Ltd, Leith	Sept 1943

Displacement, tons: 1,118 light; 1,630 full
load
Dimensions, feet (metres): 190.0 pp;
205.0 oa × 40.2 × 16.8 (58; 62.5 × 12.3 × 5.1)
Main engines: 2 Atlas Polar 8-cylinder
diesels; 1 shaft; 4,000 bhp = 16 knots
Oil fuel, tons: 405
Range, imiles: 17,000
Complement: 42

Last of a class of eight. *Reward* of this class

was brought forward from reserve in 1975
and fitted with a 40-mm gun for offshore
patrol duties. She was sunk in collision in the
Forth in 1976, salvaged in August of that
year and paid off for disposal. The
remainder of the class had eventful careers.
Growler was put on long-term charter as
Caroline Moller, renamed *Castle Peak*,
returned to the Royal Fleet Auxiliary Service
in 1957, renamed *Welshman* on charter to
United Towing Co Ltd and then *Cyclone* on

return to the RFAS in 1964. *Reward* and
Turmoil were both on charter for a time, the
former to United Towing and the latter to
Overseas Towing and Salvage. *Mediator*
was paid off in 1964 and sold to Greece in
1968, *Turmoil* was sold in 1965 and *Warden*
deleted in 1969. *Hesperia* was lost during
World War II while *Bustler* and *Samsonia*
were paid off in the mid 1970s. *Cyclone* now
at Gibraltar.

Type: Harbour Tug   *Class:* "Director"

Name	No.	Builders	Commissioned
FAITHFUL	A 85	Yarrow & Sons Ltd	1958
FORCEFUL	A 66	Yarrow & Sons Ltd	1958
FAVOURITE	A 87	Ferguson & Co Ltd	1959
DEXTEROUS	A 93	Yarrow & Sons Ltd	1957
DIRECTOR	A 94	Yarrow & Sons Ltd	1957

Displacement, tons: 710 full load
Dimensions, feet (metres): 157.2 oa × 30 (60 over paddle boxes) × 10 (47.9 × 9.2 (18.4) × 3.1)
Main engines: Paxman diesels and BTH motors; diesel electric; 2 shafts; 2 paddle wheels; 2,000 bhp = 13 knots
Complement: 21

The only class of paddle tugs operated by any navy. They have diesel-electric chain drive, side-paddles and a hinged foremast.

Originally a class of seven – *Grinder* and *Griper* deleted 1975. Their design was considered particularly effective for handling aircraft carriers.

Forceful

Type: Harbour Tug   *Class:* "Dog"

Name
AIREDALE A 102
ALSATIAN A 106
CAIRN A 126
DALMATIAN A 129
DEERHOUND A 155
ELKHOUND A 162
LABRADOR A 168
HUSKY A 169
MASTIFF A 180
SALUKI A 182
SEALYHAM A 187
POINTER A 188
SETTER A 189
SPANIEL A 201
SHEEPDOG A 250
BASSET (ex-*Beagle*) A 327
COLLIER A 328
CORGI A 330
FOXHOUND (ex-*Boxer*) A 394

Displacement, tons: 170 full load
Dimensions, feet (metres): 94 × 24.5 × 12 (28.7 × 7.5 × 3.7)
Main engines: Lister Blackstone diesels; 1,320 bhp = 12 knots
Complement: 8

Medium berthing tugs with a bollard pull of 16 tons. Completed 1962-72. *Airedale* and *Sealy Ham* at Gilbraltar. *Foxhound* renamed 22 October 1977 to free the name *Boxer* for the new Type 22 frigate.

Type: Harbour Tug   *Class:* "Girl"

Name
ALICE A 113
AGATHA A 116
AUDREY A 117
AGNES A 121
BRIDGET A 322
BETTY A 323
BARBARA A 324
BRENDA A 335

Displacement, tons: 40
Main engines: 495 bhp = 10 knots

"A" names built by PK Harris, "B" names by
Dunstons. Completed 1962-72.

Audrey △

▽ Bridget

Type: Tug | *Class:* "Modified Girl"

Name
DAISY A 145
EDITH A 177
CHARLOTTE A 210
CHRISTINE A 217
CLARE A 218
DORIS A 252
DAPHNE
DOROTHY

Displacement, tons: 38
Main engines: 495 bhp = 10 knots

"C" names built by Pimblott and "D" and "E" names by Dunstons. Completed 1972.

Celia sold to Serebawang Dockyard, Singapore in 1971.

Type: Water-Tractor | *Class:* "Triton"

Name
IRENE
ISABEL
JOAN
JOYCE
KATHLEEN
KITTY
LESLEY
LILAH
MARY
MYRTLE
NANCY
NORAH

Displacement, tons: 107.5
Main engines: 330 bhp = 8 knots

Water-Tractors with small wheel house and funnel. All completed by Dunstons by August 1974.

Isabel

Type: Water-Tractor | *Class:* "Felicity"

Name
FELICITY
FIONA
GEORGINA
GWENDOLINE
HELEN

Displacement, tons: 80
Main engines: 600 bhp = 10 knots

Water-Tractors. *Felicity* built by Dunstons, remainder by Hancocks. Completed 1973.

Helen

Type: Fleet Tender

Class: "Insect"

Name	No.	Builders	Commissioned
BEE	—	C. D. Holmes Ltd, Beverley, Yorks	1970
CICALA	—	C. D. Holmes Ltd, Beverley, Yorks	1971
COCKCHAFER	—	C. D. Holmes Ltd, Beverley, Yorks	1971
CRICKET	—	C. D. Holmes Ltd, Beverley, Yorks	1972
GNAT	—	C. D. Holmes Ltd, Beverley, Yorks	1972
LADYBIRD	—	C. D. Holmes Ltd, Beverley, Yorks	1973
SCARAB	—	C. D. Holmes Ltd, Beverley, Yorks	1973

Displacement, tons: 450 full load
Dimensions, feet (metres):
111.8 oa × 28 × 11 (34.1 × 8.5 × 3.4)
Main engines: Lister-Blackstone Diesel;
1 shaft; 660 bhp = 10.5 knots

Complement: 10

The first three of this class were fitted as store carriers with two cranes, the second three as armament-stores carriers with one crane and *Scarab* as a mooring vessel with a 3-ton crane and capable of lifting 10 tons over the bow.

Bee

Type: Diving Tender
Class: "Cartmel"

Name	No.	Builders	Commissioned
ETTRICK	A 274	J. Cook, Wivenhoe	1972
ELSING	A 277	J. Cook, Wivenhoe	1971
EPWORTH	A 352	J. Cook, Wivenhoe	1972
ELKSTONE	A 353	J. Cook, Wivenhoe	1971
FROXFIELD	A 354	R. Dunston, Thorne	1972
FELSTED	A 384	R. Dunston, Thorne	1972
DUNSTER	A 393	R. Dunston, Thorne	1972
HOLMWOOD	A 1772	R. Dunston, Thorne	1973
HORNING	A 1773	R. Dunston, Thorne	1973
CARTMEL	—	I. Pimblott & Sons, Northwich	1971
CAWSAND	—	I. Pimblott & Sons, Northwich	1971
CRICCIETH	—	I. Pimblott & Sons, Northwich	1972
CRICKLADE	—	C. D. Holmes, Beverley	1971
CROMARTY	—	J. Lewis, Aberdeen	1972
DENMEAD	—	C. D. Holmes, Beverley	1972
DORNOCH	—	J. Lewis, Aberdeen	1972
FINTRY	—	J. Lewis, Aberdeen	1972
FOTHERBY	—	R. Dunston, Thorne	1972
FULBECK	—	C. D. Holmes, Beverley	1972
GLENCOVE	—	I. Pimblott & Sons, Northwich	1972
GRASMERE	—	J. Lewis, Aberdeen	1972
HAMBLEDON	—	R. Dunston, Thorne	1973
HARLECH	—	R. Dunston, Thorne	1973
HEADCORN	—	R. Dunston, Thorne	1973
HEVER	—	R. Dunston, Thorne	1973
LAMLASH	—	R. Dunston, Thorne	1974
LECHLADE	—	R. Dunston, Thorne	1974
LLANDOVERY	—	R. Dunston, Thorne	1974

Displacement, tons: 143 full load
Dimensions, feet (metres): 80 oa × 21 × 6.6
(24.1 × 6.4 × 3)
Main engines: 1 Lister-Blackstone diesel;
1 shaft; 320 bhp = 10.5 knots
Complement: 6

An improved "Aberdovey" class of three

variants – cargo only, passenger or cargo,
training tenders (complement of 12). *Elsing*
and *Ettrick* (RN manned) at Gibraltar.

Epworth

Type: Fleet Tender   *Class:* "Aberdovey"

Name	No.	Builders	Commissioned
ABERDOVEY	—	Isaac Pimblott & Sons, Northwich	1963
ABINGER	—	Isaac Pimblott & Sons, Northwich	1964
ALNESS	—	Isaac Pimblott & Sons, Northwich	1965
ALNMOUTH	—	Isaac Pimblott & Sons, Northwich	1966
APPLEBY	—	Isaac Pimblott & Sons, Northwich	1967
ASHCOTT	—	Isaac Pimblott & Sons, Northwich	1968
BEAULIEU	A 99	J. S. Doig, Grimsby	1966
BEDDGELERT	A 100	J. S. Doig, Grimsby	1967
BEMBRIDGE	A 101	J. S. Doig, Grimsby	1968
BIBURY	A 103	J. S. Doig, Grimsby	1969
BLAKENEY	A 104	J. S. Doig, Grimsby	1970
BRODICK	A 105	J. S. Doig, Grimsby	1971

Displacement, tons: 117.5 full load
Dimensions, feet (metres):
79.8 oa × 18 × 5.5 (24 × 5.4 × 2.4)
Main engines: 1 Lister-Blackstone diesel;
1 shaft; 225 bhp = 10.5 knots

Complement: 6

The first post-war design of fleet tenders. Carry 25 tons or 200 standing passengers as well as two torpedoes. *Alnmouth*

operates from Devonport for the Sea Cadet Corps, *Aberdovey* works with Royal Marines, Poole.

Bembridge

Type: Diving Tender   *Class:* "Cartmel"

Name	No.	Builders	Commissioned
IRONBRIDGE (ex-*Invergordon*)	A 310	Gregson Ltd, Blyth	1974
IXWORTH	A 318	Gregson Ltd, Blyth	1974
CLOVELLY	A 389	I. Pimblott & Sons, Northwich	1972
ILCHESTER	—	Gregson Ltd, Blyth	1974
INSTOW	—	Gregson Ltd, Blyth	1974

Displacement, tons: 143 full load
Dimensions, feet (metres): 80 oa × 21 × 6.6
(24.1 × 6.4 × 3)
Main engines: 1 Lister-Blackstone diesel;

1 shaft; 320 bhp = 10.5 knots
Complement: 6

Of same class as "Cartmel" tenders.

RN manned. "Datchet" of approximately the same size but different externally also operates as a diving tender.

Ixworth △   ▽ Portisham

Type: RNXS Tender

Class: "Ham"

Name
PAGHAM M 2716
SHIPHAM M 2726
THAKEHAM M 2733
TONGHAM M 2735
PORTISHAM M 2781
PUTTENHAM M 2784

Displacement, tons: 120 standard; 159 full load
Dimensions, feet (metres): 2601 Series: 100 pp; 106.5 oa × 21.2 × 5.5 (30.5; 32.4 × 6.5 × 1.7); 2793 Series: 100 pp;

107.5 oa × 22 × 5.8 (30.5; 32.1 × 6.6 × 1.8)
Main engines: 2 Paxman diesels; 1,100 bhp = 14 knots
Oil fuel, tons: 15
Complement: 15 (2 officers and 13 ratings)

Converted from Inshore Minesweepers in 1960s. Due for replacement by the "Loyal" class.

Type: Tender   *Class:* "Loyal"

Name
LOYAL MODERATOR A 220
VIGILANT (ex-*Loyal Factor*) A 382
ALERT (ex-*Loyal Governor*) A 510
LOYAL PROCTOR A 1771
LOYAL CHANCELLOR
LOYAL HELPER

Displacement, tons: 143 full load
Dimensions, feet (metres): 80 oa × 21 × 6.6 (24.1 × 6.4 × 3)
Main engines: 1 Lister-Blackstone diesel; 1 shaft; 320 bhp = 10.5 knots

Complement: 6

Of similar characteristics to the "Cartmel" class. Originally intended for the Royal Naval Auxiliary Service at Portland, *Loyal*

Moderator is in use for harbour training at Plymouth while *Loyal Governor* (renamed *Alert*) and *Loyal Factor* (renamed Vigilant) are employed by the RN on patrol duties off Northern Ireland. Four more on order.

Loyal Moderator

Type: Degaussing Vessel   *Class:* "Ham"

Name
FORDHAM M 2717
WARMINGHAM M 2737
THATCHAM M 2790

Displacement, tons: 120 standard; 159 full load
Dimensions, feet (metres): 2601 Series: 100 pp; 106.5 oa × 21.2 × 5.5 (30.5; 32.4 × 6.5 × 1.7) 2793 Series: 100 pp;

107.5 oa × 22 × 5.8 (30.5; 32.1 × 6.6 × 1.8)
Main engines: 2 Paxman diesels; 1,100 bhp = 14 knots
Oil fuel, tons: 15
Complement: 15 (2 officers and 13 ratings)

A type of conversion of the Inshore Minesweepers put into effect in the late 1960s.

Warmingham

Type: Trawler (TCV)   *Class:* "Isles"

Name	No.	Builders	Commissioned
CALDY	A 332	John Lewis and Sons	1943
BERN	A 334	Cook Welton and Gemmell	1942
LUNDY	A 336	Cook Welton and Gemmell	1943
SKOMER	A 338	John Lewis and Sons	1943
GRAEMSAY	A 340	Ardrossan Dockyard Co	1943
SWITHA	A 346	A. and J. Inglis Ltd	1942

Displacement, tons: 770 full load
Dimensions, feet (metres):
164 oa × 27.5 × 14 (49 × 8.4 × 4.2)
Main engines: Triple expansion; 1 shaft;
850 ihp = 12 knots
Boiler: 1 cylindrical

Coal, tons: 183

These six ships are the last survivors in the RN of a class of 145 built during the war for minesweeping and escort duties. Of those available in 1945-46 most were converted

for wreck dispersal duties. Nine of these ships being converted for tank-cleaning in the mid-1950s. *Bardsey* was transferred to Malta Dockyard and *Foulness* deleted in 1973 and *Coll* in 1977.

Type: Scottish Fishery Protection Vessel   *Class:* "Jura"

Name	No.	Builders	Commissioned
JURA	—	Hall, Russell & Co. Aberdeen	1973
WESTRA	—	Hall, Russell & Co, Aberdeen	1975

Displacement, tons: 778 light; 1,285 full
load
Measurement, tonsA 942 gross
Dimensions, feet (metres):
195.3 oa × 35 × 14.4 × (59.6 × 10.7 × 4.4)
Main engines: 2 British Polar SP112VS-F
diesels; 4,200 bhp; 1 shaft = 17 knots
Complement: 28

These two ships were built for the Department of Agriculture and Fisheries for Scotland. In the Defence Estimates 1975 it was stated that *Jura* was being taken over temporarily on loan from that Department for off-shore patrol duties. For this purpose she was fitted with a 40-mm gun and, with pennant number P296, she operated as

such until returned by MOD(N) in January 1977, shortly after *Jersey* had been commissioned. *Westra* was launched on 6 August 1974. Three other smaller craft are operated by the Scottish Office.

A number of MFVs are used in dockyard ports, not necessarily under naval control. In addition to the ships of the Royal Navy, Royal Fleet Auxiliary Service and Royal Maritime Auxiliary Service a number of ships and craft are operated by the Royal Corps of Transport and the Royal Air Force.

Royal Corps of Transport
1 "Ham" class – *RG Masters*
1 90 ft MFV – *Yarmouth Navigator*

1 GS Launch (72 ft) – *Trevose*
7 GS Launches (50 ft) – *Jackson, Martin, Newman Noggs, Oliver Twist, Raddle, Smike, Uriah Heep.*
7 GD Launches (47 ft) (WB01-7) – *Carp, Chub, Bream, Barbel, Roach, Perch, Pike*
6 Command Craft (41 ft) (L01-6) – *Fulmar, Petrel, Shearwater, Shelduck, Skua, Tern.*
2 Ex-SAR craft *Minora, Hyperion.*

Royal Air Force
3 LRRSC "Seal" class – *Seal, Sea Gull, Sea Otter*
4 RTTL Mk3 "Spitfire" class – *Spitfire, Sunderland, Stirling, Halifax*
4 RTTL Mk2 – 2752, 2757, 2768, 2771
10 "1300" Series Pinnaces
7 "1600" Series Range Safety Launches

Harbour Craft – 24 ft tenders and Gemini craft being replaced by Cheverton Workboats.

Armaments and Equipment

During World War II and the next fifteen years or so the Royal Navy was equipped with "guns", "torpedoes", "sonar", "radar" and the rest. After the early 1960s these were replaced by "weapon systems". The change in title was most significant. It meant the end of the Gunnery Control officer bellowing "up 400 – Zig Zag – Shoot", the series of orders to the depth-charges as the Asdic/Sonar reported "instant echoes" – detection devices, weapons and ships could be conjoined by modern communications and, later, by the output of a computer.

As a result of this very complete jump forward in technology the reaction time of a ship's weapons became far less than had been dreamed of. By the mid-1960s ships could exchange data at a speed unthought of in the days of the Aldis lamp and the interminable "Say again" on ship-to-ship VHF circuits. But this was necessary in an era when aircraft speeds had gone from 500 knots to Mach 1.5, missiles of similar speeds were at sea and when submarines could move at dived speeds of 25 knots rather than 10, or at the most 16. At the same time the helicopter had entered the lists; as a submarine detector, as submarine killer, as a missile director or as a straightforward reconnaissance machine. Things had speeded up to a degree which

required highly complicated electronic devices to aid the command in making correct decisions, whether it was a minesweeper or a fleet which depended on the outcome.

At the same time as detection devices were improved so were their counters. Radar detection of a ship could be out-ranged by SHF D/F detection of the radar transmissions, sonar impulses could be heard by a submarine well beyond the certain detection range of the transmitting set, even radar could be jammed effectively. What has resulted from these various combinations is the need for a highly professional thought-process at command level which must not only take account of own capabilities but also be influenced by intelligence of the enemy's material condition and his likely tactics. This can be greatly assisted by computers on board but the final result inevitably depends on a man-made decision.

These are a few of the thoughts which should be in one's mind when looking at a modern warship. The huge aerials of the air-search radars, the complexity of the variable depth sonar, the astonishing agility of modern missile mountings are inclined to bemuse one's facilities but the man behind all these technical marvels will, for many years ahead, be the prime factor.

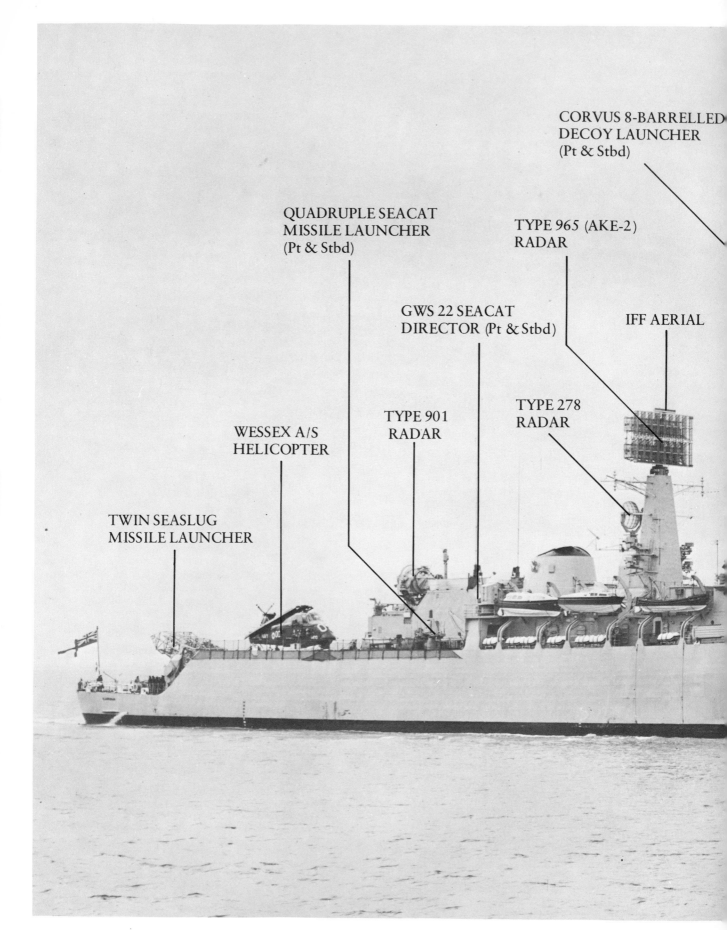

CORVUS 8-BARRELLED
DECOY LAUNCHER
(Pt & Stbd)

QUADRUPLE SEACAT
MISSILE LAUNCHER
(Pt & Stbd)

TYPE 965 (AKE-2)
RADAR

GWS 22 SEACAT
DIRECTOR (Pt & Stbd)

IFF AERIAL

WESSEX A/S
HELICOPTER

TYPE 901
RADAR

TYPE 278
RADAR

TWIN SEASLUG
MISSILE LAUNCHER

HMS Glamorgan
"County" class light cruiser

SINGLE 20-mm
OERLIKON GUN
(Pt & Stbd)

TYPE 992
RADAR

TYPE 975
RADAR

M/F DF
AERIAL

MRS 3 GUNNERY
DIRECTOR

FOUR EXOCET MISSILE
LAUNCHERS

TWIN 4.5-in GUN
Mk 6

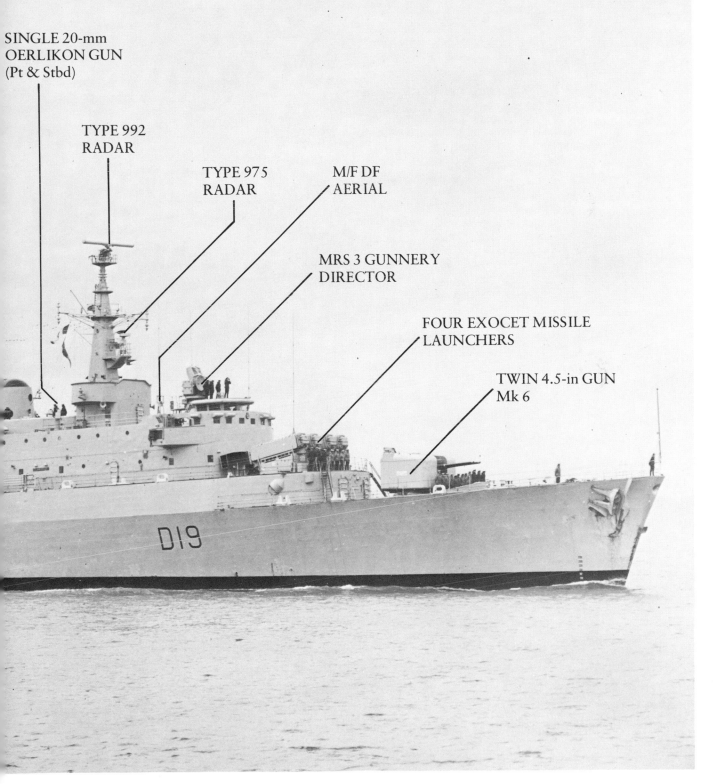

D19

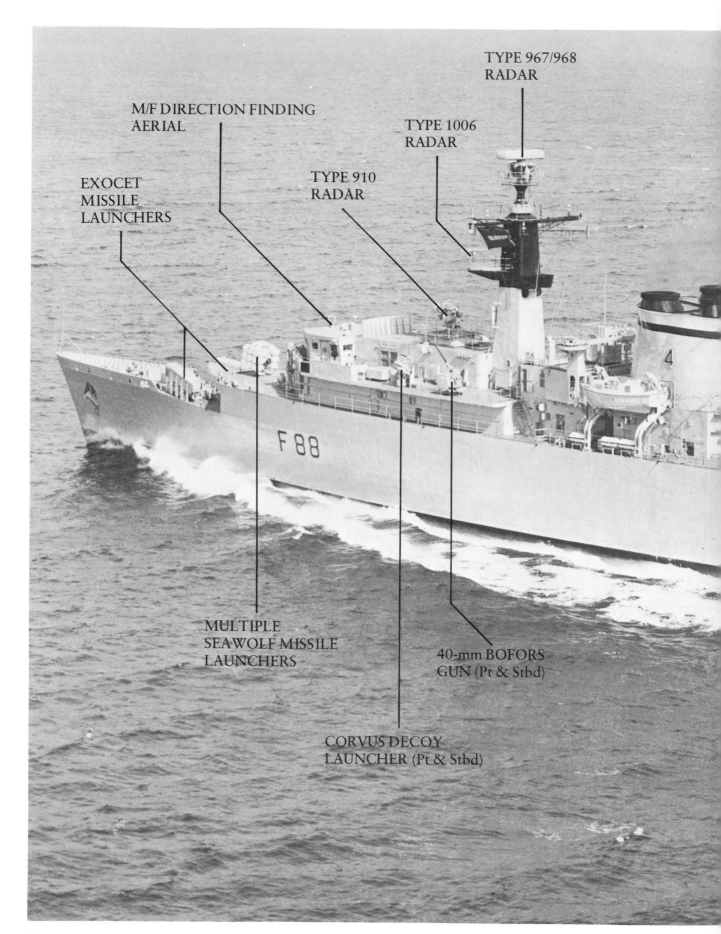

TYPE 967/968
RADAR

M/F DIRECTION FINDING
AERIAL

TYPE 1006
RADAR

TYPE 910
RADAR

EXOCET
MISSILE
LAUNCHERS

F88

MULTIPLE
SEAWOLF MISSILE
LAUNCHERS

40-mm BOFORS
GUN (Pt & Stbd)

CORVUS DECOY
LAUNCHER (Pt & Stbd)

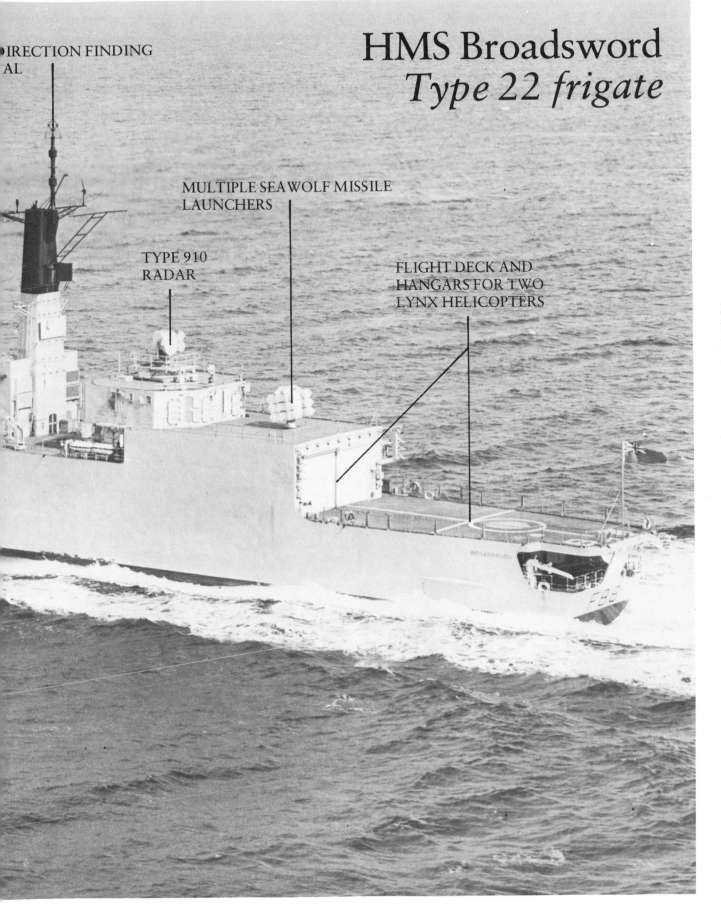

IRECTION FINDING
AL

HMS Broadsword
Type 22 frigate

MULTIPLE SEAWOLF MISSILE
LAUNCHERS

TYPE 910
RADAR

FLIGHT DECK AND
HANGARS FOR TWO
LYNX HELICOPTERS

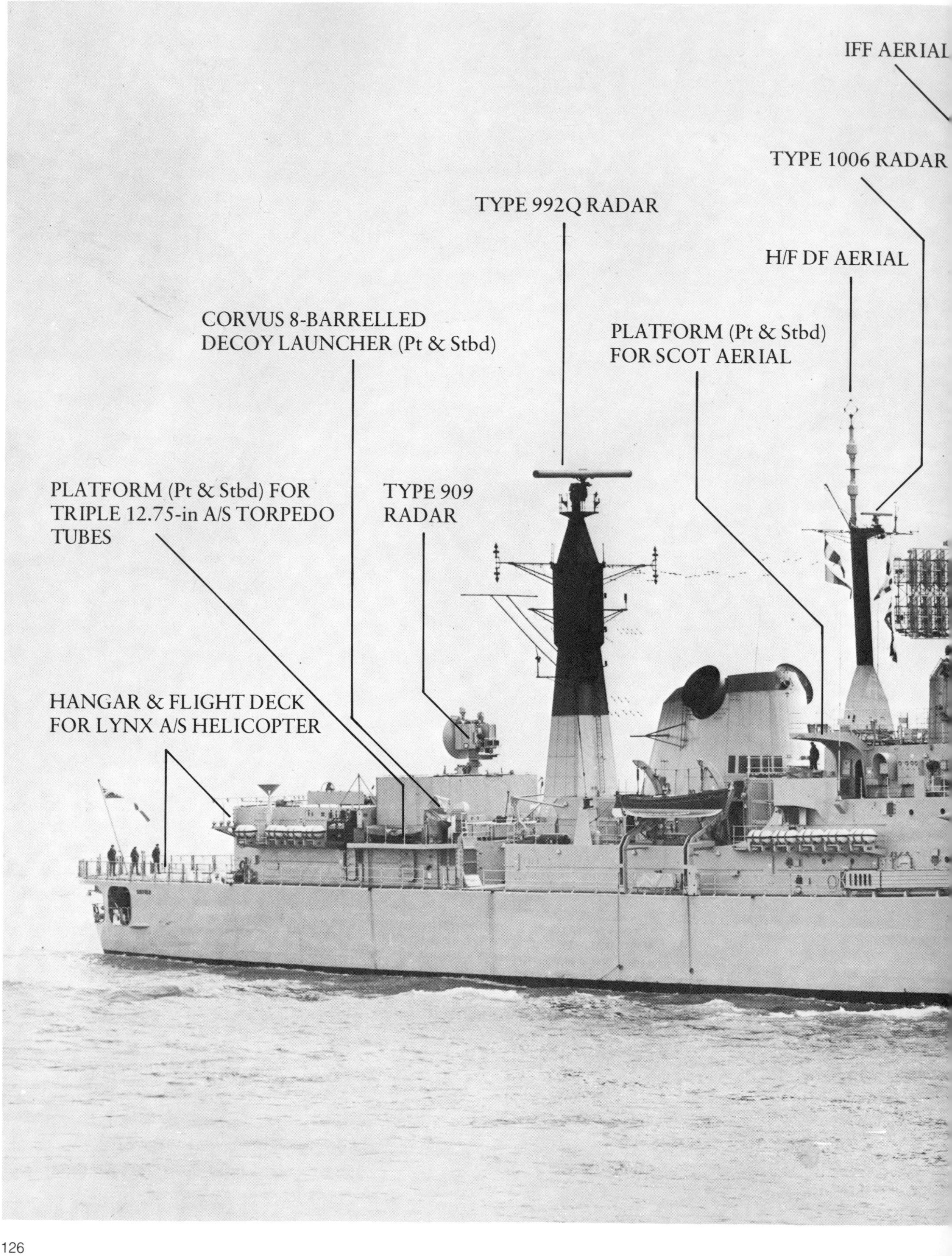

IFF AERIAL

TYPE 1006 RADAR

TYPE 992Q RADAR

H/F DF AERIAL

CORVUS 8-BARRELLED
DECOY LAUNCHER (Pt & Stbd)

PLATFORM (Pt & Stbd)
FOR SCOT AERIAL

PLATFORM (Pt & Stbd) FOR
TRIPLE 12.75-in A/S TORPEDO
TUBES

TYPE 909
RADAR

HANGAR & FLIGHT DECK
FOR LYNX A/S HELICOPTER

HMS Sheffield
Type 42 destroyer

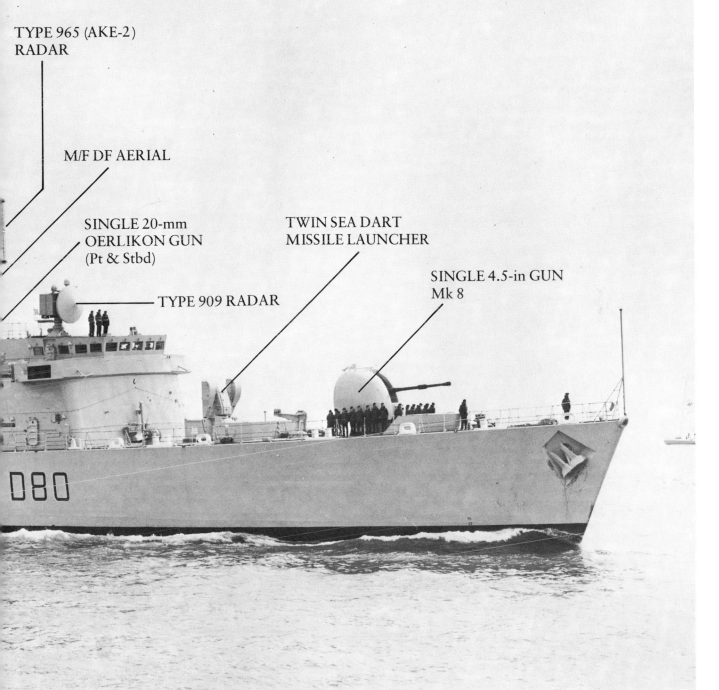

TYPE 965 (AKE-2)
RADAR

M/F DF AERIAL

SINGLE 20-mm
OERLIKON GUN
(Pt & Stbd)

TYPE 909 RADAR

TWIN SEA DART
MISSILE LAUNCHER

SINGLE 4.5-in GUN
Mk 8

D80

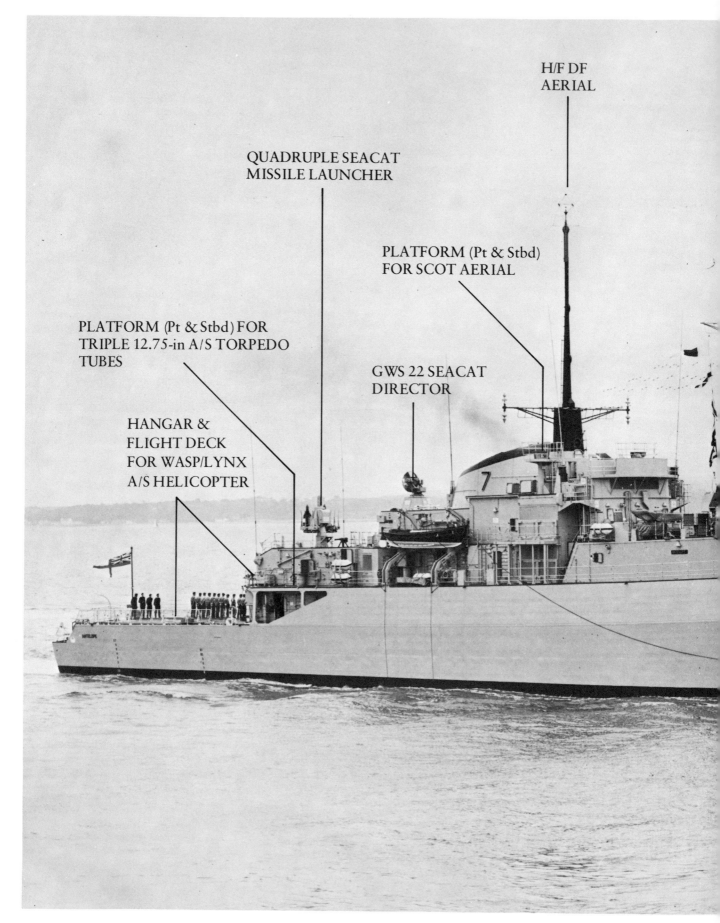

H/F DF
AERIAL

QUADRUPLE SEACAT
MISSILE LAUNCHER

PLATFORM (Pt & Stbd)
FOR SCOT AERIAL

PLATFORM (Pt & Stbd) FOR
TRIPLE 12.75-in A/S TORPEDO
TUBES

GWS 22 SEACAT
DIRECTOR

HANGAR &
FLIGHT DECK
FOR WASP/LYNX
A/S HELICOPTER

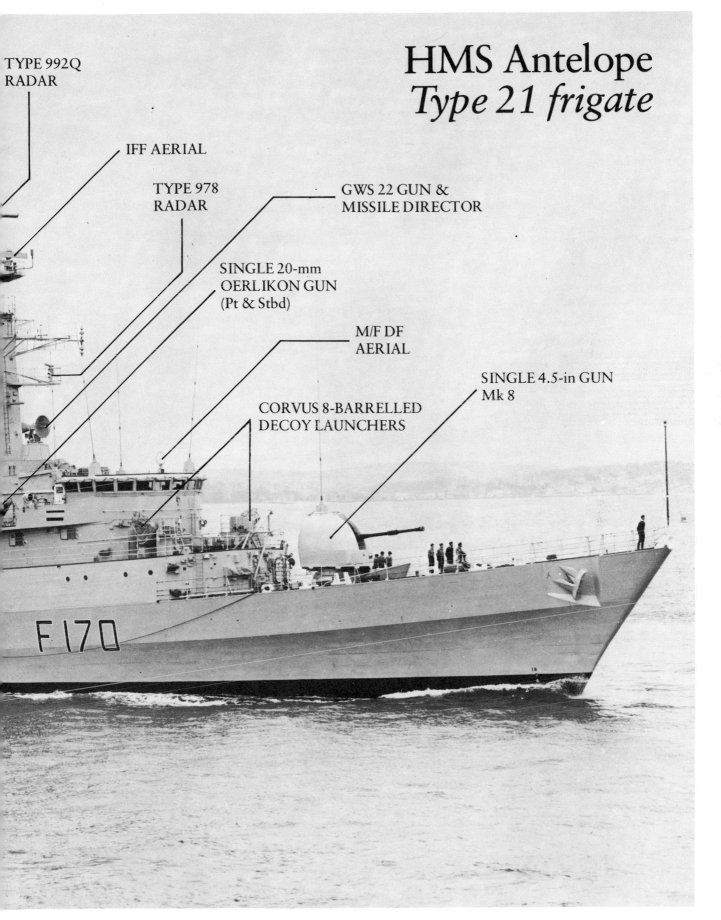

TYPE 992Q
RADAR

IFF AERIAL

TYPE 978
RADAR

GWS 22 GUN &
MISSILE DIRECTOR

SINGLE 20-mm
OERLIKON GUN
(Pt & Stbd)

M/F DF
AERIAL

SINGLE 4.5-in GUN
Mk 8

CORVUS 8-BARRELLED
DECOY LAUNCHERS

HMS Antelope
Type 21 frigate

F 170

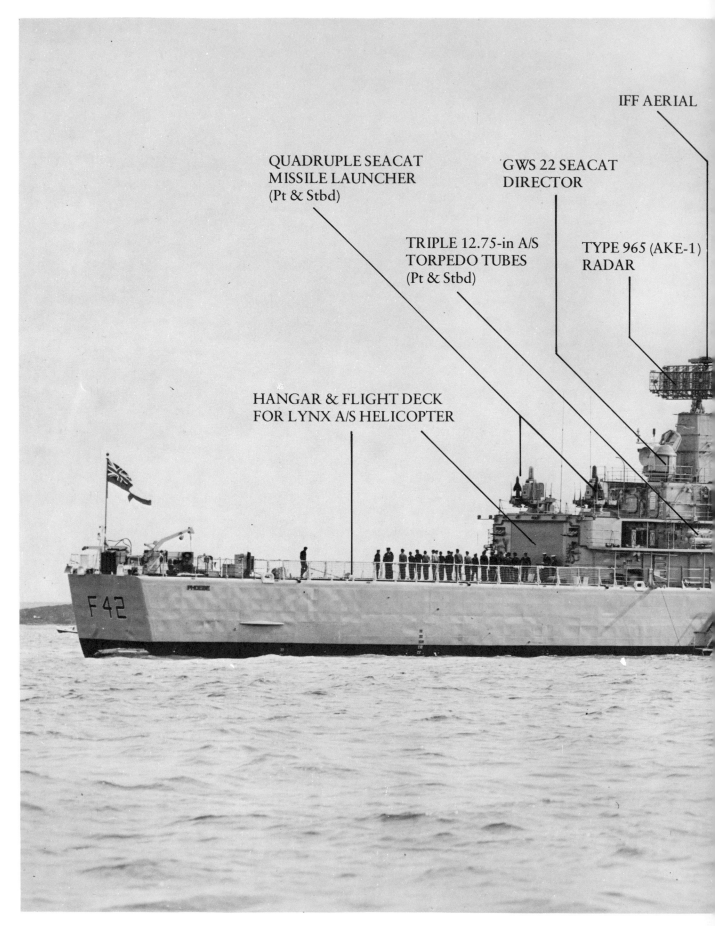

IFF AERIAL

QUADRUPLE SEACAT
MISSILE LAUNCHER
(Pt & Stbd)

GWS 22 SEACAT
DIRECTOR

TRIPLE 12.75-in A/S
TORPEDO TUBES
(Pt & Stbd)

TYPE 965 (AKE-1)
RADAR

HANGAR & FLIGHT DECK
FOR LYNX A/S HELICOPTER

F 42

PHOEBE

HMS Phoebe
"Leander" class frigate

CORVUS
8-BARRELLED DECOY
LAUNCHER

SCOT AERIAL
(Pt & Stbd)

TYPE 993 RADAR

TYPE 975
RADAR

M/F DF AERIAL

GWS 22 SEACAT
DIRECTOR

SINGLE 40-mm BOFORS
GUN (Pt & Stbd)

FOUR EXOCET
MISSILE LAUNCHERS

F42

Glossary of Equipment

AIRCRAFT

Westland/Aérospatiale Lynx HAS.2
Developed for advanced shipborne anti-submarine and other duties. Equipped with Ferranti Seaspray search and tracking radar, Lynx carries a variety of armament, including Mk 44 or Mk 46 homing torpedoes; Mk 11 depth charges or Sea Skua semi-active homing missiles. Powered by two 900-shp Rolls-Royce Gem Turboshafts, Lynx has a maximum speed of 145 kt, a radius of action of 136 nm and weighs 10,500 lb fully laden.

Westland Wasp HAS.1
First entered service in 1963 and operates in the anti-submarine role from "Leander", "Rothesay" and "Tribal" class frigates. Not equipped with detection equipment, the Wasp relies on the carrier ship for target information. Armament consists typically of two Mk 44 homing torpedoes. Powered by a single 710-shp Rolls-Royce Nimbus turboshaft, Wasp has a maximum speed of 104 kt, a radius of action of 115 nm and weighs 5,500 lb fully laden.

Westland Sea King HAS.1 and HAS.2
The first of 56 Royal Navy Sea King HAS.1s first flew in May 1969, later equipping five squadrons in the advanced anti-submarine role. Subsequently, twenty-one of the uprated HAS.2 version were ordered for ASW and SAR duties, the first of these flying for the first time in June 1976. Sea Kings can carry a wide variety of operational equipment, including (for ASW) Plessey Type 195 dipping Sonars, AW 391 search radar in a dorsal radome, two No 4 marine markers, up to four Mk 44 homing torpedoes or four Mk 11 depth charges. Powered by a pair of 1,660-shp Rolls-Royce Gnome turboshafts, the Sea King HAS.2 has a cruising speed of 112 kt, a radius of action of 330 miles and weighs 21,000 lb fully laden.

Westland Wessex HAS.1 and HAS.3
The Wessex HAS.1 entered service in July 1961 and, powered by a single 1,450-shp Napier Gazelle turboshaft, had a maximum speed of 115 kt. The Wessex HAS.3, which began to enter service in 1967, is similar to the Mk 1 but is powered by a 1,600-shp Gazelle Mk 165 and is fitted with search radar in a 'hump-back' radome. Maximum speed is 116 kt, range is 290 nm and the Wessex 3 weighs 13,600 lb fully laden.

ANTI-SUBMARINE EQUIPMENT

Acoustic Decoy
A towed noise maker designed to disturb submarines' sonars and to distract homing torpedoes.

Bathythermograph
An instrument towed over the stern to detect variations in water temperature.

Ikara
An Australian-designed anti-submarine weapon system comprising a guided solid-fuelled vehicle and an acoustic homing torpedo (such as the American Mk 44). The system is ship-controlled and has a range of 13 nm (24 km).

Limbo (AS Mk 10)
A triple-barrelled anti-submarine mortar with all-round coverage. Fully gyro-stabilised, the system has a range of about 1,000 yards (915 m). Limbo is the successor to the Squid mortar and was first introduced to Royal Navy ships in the early 1960s.

Torpedo Tubes
12.75-in tubes for American Mk 44 or Mk 46 anti-submarine torpedoes. The Mk 44 is an obsolescent ship- or air-launched acoustic-homing torpedo; the Mk 46 is the successor to the Mk 44 and uses active/passive acoustic homing. Warhead weight for both is about 88 lb (40 kg).

VDS
Variable Depth Sonar; Type 199. This utilises a sonar transducer towed in a closed body behind and below the operating ship, the purpose being to enable the detecting device to operate at various levels and therefore overcome the refractive effect of temperature gradients in the sea.

COMMUNICATIONS EQUIPMENT

H/F.DF
A direction-finding device for high-frequency transmissions.

M/F.DF
A direction-finding device for medium-frequency transmissions.

SCOT
Satellite Communications Onboard Terminal.

GUNNERY

Corvus Launcher
An eight-barrelled launcher for flares, or 'Chaff' (*Window*) as a jammer, particularly for anti-shipping missile homing heads.

Gun 4.5-in Mk 6
A twin-barrelled turret developed in 1946. Maximum range is about 10 nm (19 km) and rate of fire up to 20 rounds per barrel per minute.

Gun 4.5-in Mk 8
A fully-automatic single-barrelled gun based on the Army's Abbott gun and introduced in 1971. Maximum range about 12 nm (22 km) and rate of fire 25 rounds per minute.

Twin 40-mm (Bofors) Mounting Mk 5
The 60-calibre version was first introduced in 1942 and is used for close-range engagements. Maximum rate of fire is 120 rounds per minute per barrel, and tactical range is 3 km.

Single 40-mm (Bofors) Mounting Mk 7
The Mk 7 uses the 70-calibre gun, first introduced in 1946. Maximum rate of fire is 300 rounds per minute with a tactical range of 4 km.

Single 20-mm (Oerlikon) Mounting Type GAM-B
A short-range gun equally suitable for surface-to-surface engagements or, with a tactical range of up to 1,500 m, for anti-aircraft defence. Rate of fire up to 1,000 rounds per minute.

GUNNERY/MISSILE CONTROL

GWS 22
Control system for Seacat missiles and, in Type 21 Frigates, for gunnery control.

MRS 3
Control system for 4.5-in guns.

MISSILES

MM 38 Exocet
A surface-to-surface tactical missile with a range of approximately 23 nm (42 km), propelled by a two-stage solid-fuel motor. Warhead weight is approximately 363 lb (165 kg) of high explosive.

Seacat
A close-range shipborne missile for anti-aircraft defence, but which can also be used against surface targets within visual range. Maximum effective range is about 4,350 yards (4,750 m) and the warhead is high explosive.

Sea Dart
Designated GWS 30, Sea Dart is a third-generation area defence weapon system capable of intercepting high- and low-flying aircraft, and air- and surface-launched missiles. Powered by a solid-fuel booster and ramjet sustainer, Sea Dart has a range of at least 16 nm (30 km). Warhead is high explosive.

Seaslug
An obsolescent long-range beam-riding surface-to-air missile. There are two versions of the missile, the Mk 2 having longer range (better than 24 nm (45 km) and better performance against low-flying aircraft. Both missiles also have a surface-to-surface capability.

Seawolf
This missile is used in the GWS 25 short-range self-defence missile system for use against both aircraft and anti-ship missiles. Propulsion is by solid-fuel motor and the warhead is high explosive.

RADARS

Type 268
Surface search. Now obsolete.

278
Nodding height-finder.

901
Target tracking and missile guidance for the Seaslug shipborne surface-to-air missile system.

909
Target tracking and illumination for the Sea Dart air defence missile.

910
Radar tracking element of the Seawolf point defence missile system. Surveillance and target designation data are provided by the Types 967 and 968 air and surface surveillance radars.

912
Royal Navy's designation for the Selenia Orion RTN-10X fire control radar.

965
Standard long-range air search radar of the Royal Navy. Supplied with either single or double-stacked antenna (AKE-1 or AKE-2). In addition to air surveillance, the type fulfills target designation functions for guided weapon systems, and IFF facilities are also provided.

967
Air surveillance radar integrated with the Type 968 surface surveillance radar to form a compact short- to medium-range defence radar. Together with the Type 910 Target Tracker, they form the radar group for the Seawolf system.

968
See above.

975
Lightweight high definition surface warning radar for smaller warships. Primarily for navigation, it can also be adapted for minehunting, in which configuration it is designated Type 975 ZW.

978
Navigation radar for frigates and larger ships.

992
Obsolescent long-range surveillance radar.

992Q
High power surface search radar providing the prime source of target information for the Action Information Organisation system on board destroyers and frigates.

993
Tactical air search radar.

994
Type 993 antenna linked to new transmitter/receiver based on the Plessey AWS-2.

1006
Navigation radar. Successor to the Type 975.

IFF
Identification Friend or Foe. Enables a radar operator to trigger a transponder in friendly aircraft to display identification marks on his radar scope.

Class Index

General Index